Dividend Investing:
A Guide to Building Sustainable Passive Income

Dedicated to my father, Jack Park, who is also a CPA and a published author

The Self Made Investor
www.theselfmadeinvestor.com

ISBN-13: 978-1-7339722-1-5
ISBN-10: 1-7339722-1-8

About the Author

James Park is a CPA who has worked in the accounting profession for a number of years. He has a BS from Franklin University and an MBA with a focus on finance from The Ohio State University. Investing has always been one of his many passions. He believes in a self-directed, low-fee approach that relies on asset allocation and rebalancing. When the right asset classes are invested in for the long-term, the odds of the stock and real estate markets are undeniably stacked in the investor's favor. When sustainable dividends are added to the mix, the investor should feel comfortable that the income will persist indefinitely. His philosophy is that investing should be simple, and good information should be available to all investors.

He lives with his caring wife, Ngouanephone Khatmay Park. She has always been supportive of his endeavors and will always serve as inspiration.

Table of Contents

Introduction

I firmly believe that every investor should focus on goals that can be accomplished. It's healthier than chasing goals that are simply beyond reach. And when it comes to investing, there's a great deal that the individual investor can accomplish. All you need is a basic understanding of how markets function, and some confidence that by investing in the right asset classes for the long-term, you'll be rewarded with strong results.

The world of investing might seem confusing at first. That's because there are a lot of high-salaried "experts" who want you to be confused. They want investors to rely on them, to feel uncomfortable out there on their own. But at the same time, there are many talented advisors who provide a tremendous service to their clients, and explain the investing world in the same terms used in this book. It's like anything else in life. There's an overwhelming amount of information at your disposal, and separating good advice from the not-so-good advice is a chore unto itself. The goal of *Dividend Investing* is not just to teach you how to build a stream of sustainable dividend income, but to help you build confidence in your investments as you pursue a low-fee, self-directed approach to building wealth.

It's important to start with realistic expectations. I'm not going to tell you that there are goals you can't accomplish, but at the same time there are limits to the amount of wealth that can be accumulated with any investment strategy. How much money you accumulate is a factor of how much you invest, how well you invest, and how long you invest. I'm a firm believer that it's important to start any endeavor with an understanding of what's realistic, and then determine if it's worth the effort. Setting realistic goals also allows you to evaluate your accomplishments along the way. It lets you know if you're making the right amount of progress. Building a portfolio for retirement (or any financial goal) is indeed a worthwhile endeavor. And if you're inclined to structure your portfolio around dividend-paying investments, then *Dividend Investing* will teach you how to build your portfolio.

Investing in dividend stocks can help you build wealth, and just as important, it can help you build a stream of income to rely on for the rest of your life. The steps are very simple and will be outlined in detail. But at a high level, all you need to do is accumulate low-fee investments that pay a dividend, reinvest those dividends for as long as you can, and wait to start spending the dividends until you're satisfied with the income they generate. *I hope this sounds like fun!* If not, then it's time to stop viewing your finances as a chore and think of it as journey. You won't build sustainable wealth overnight. But if you make some simple yet rewarding decisions, then you're on your way. After that, you simply repeat the first step over and over again until you've met your goal. I feel an endorphin rush every time I receive an email from my discount broker notifying me that another dividend has been received. It's a sense of progress. And while it might seem counterintuitive, I don't get worried when my investments decline in value. We're only going to invest in markets that have a history of beating inflation over prolonged periods of time, but they won't move up in a perfectly straight line. We will encounter market pullbacks. And we can benefit from those pullbacks. A bear market should be viewed as the dividend investor's best friend, especially when the bear is encountered early in your investment career. Watching those dividends get reinvested at deep discount bear prices transforms the agony of an economic downturn into a worthwhile excursion that sets the stage for the accumulation of long-term wealth. Of course, it's critical that you don't get scared and sell, but instead buy as much as you can.

Within these pages we'll discuss much more than just the benefits of nabbing bargains during a bear market. In fact, if we drop our eggs into enough baskets then the pains of a bear market won't even faze us. All we have to do is diversify, learn to recognize the characteristics that make for a sustainable dividend, and of course, maintain a lifestyle that affords us the savings we need to build our investments. These are important concepts, and we'll cover them with the goal of dividend accumulation as the centerpiece.

But I do need to warn you—*this is not your typical book on dividend investing*. There are plenty of books that teach you how to select dividend-paying stocks. And those books are filled with valuable information. We're going to cover some of the same material here. But this is not purely a book on selecting dividend stocks. Rather, it's a book about portfolio construction for the dividend-minded investor. We like dividends because of the impact that compounding has on our portfolio, plain and simple. All else being equal, it's better to receive a dividend than to not receive a dividend. But we also like capital gains. And where we can get substantial capital gains at the expense of a couple points in dividend yield, we'll take it. Index funds that provide capital gains over dividends are a useful tool for increasing the size of the portfolio, which in turn increases our dividend income over the long-haul. If that sounds confusing, don't worry about it, there's a separate chapter dedicated to each of these concepts, including a chapter on how to pick dividend stocks. If that's why you're here, to learn more about picking stocks, then I've got you covered. When we find an individual stock that not only hints at above average returns, but suggests an annual increase to the dividend payment, we're going to buy it. But we are not going to construct a portfolio focused on individual stocks. Instead, we're going to construct the portfolio around index funds, and then add some very carefully selected dividend stocks to the portfolio in an effort to get a leg over the market. Even if it's just a little bit, it helps more than most investors realize, because dividend payments are recurring. If we can get just a little extra without increasing our risk, the benefits will keep multiplying over our investment horizon. We'll see how that extra hair of a return compounds over thirty years, and provides an extra $100,000 (*or more!*) at retirement.

I hope this sounds exciting. And I hope it sounds achievable. Because it's important to focus on goals that can be accomplished. At the same time, it's also important to have realistic expectations. The strategies discussed within aren't going to make you abundantly rich in a short period of time. It's not that the strategies have shortcomings, but that the wants and desires of the typical investor exceed those of what a realistic return can provide. This book is not going to encourage you to take on large amounts of risk in search of some extravagant return. When we assume ever riskier positions in hopes of achieving ever grander rewards, we become our own worst enemy. This book will teach you to do just the opposite. Controlling for risk is paramount to a successful strategy. Like all investors, the dividend aficionado wants to maximize their returns while minimizing their risk. Diversification and asset allocation should be at the cornerstone of every investment strategy. So let's plan on throwing some bonds and real estate into the portfolio. Dividends are great, but interest and rents serve an equivalent purpose, and for all extends and purposes (other than the tax implications), those distributions are no different than a dividend. So we'll spend some time discussing bonds and

REITs, and then we'll take a look at how a properly structured portfolio allows different asset classes to work in tandem.

While it would be great to focus purely on the attributes that make for a reliable dividend, and then buy as many stocks as possible that posses such attributes, our strategy is slightly more sophisticated, yet exponentially more beneficial. We like dividends because they allow us to compound our returns. As we accumulate wealth this will be a powerful tool. And once we're ready to enjoy that wealth, our dividends will serve as a stream of income rather than a tool for compounding. The benefits of dividend income are truly two-fold, and their use will change as we progress through our investment horizon.

The great thing about dividends is that they provide a source of income that lasts indefinitely. The ability to receive a distribution without having to deplete the number of shares held is a powerful ally. And continuing to receive that distribution in perpetuity is even better. Not every company is going to pay their dividend forever, but a well-diversified portfolio that's heavily weighted toward dividend paying stocks, bonds, and REITs will provide a consistent stream of income for as long as you hold the assets.

And while this is all going to be fun and exciting, it's important to reiterate that *this book is not going to make you rich overnight*. It could very possibly make you rich at some point in your life, but that takes a lot dedication on your part. This book won't make you a millionaire by the end of the year, and perhaps not even in the next five years. If that's a problem, don't worry, there are plenty of books out there aimed at selling the millionaire dream. Some of them are realistic approaches that teach you to build wealth over time as markets move through their cycles and provide long-term returns that are consistent with expectations based on historical averages. Other books promise a quick route to riches, oftentimes with the requirement that you take out loans and assume leveraged positions that are anything but safe. And some books will advocate taking on short positions in an effort to predict market direction. I'm not an advocate of debt financed (otherwise known as leveraged) positions, because what promises above average returns on the upside will also provide above average losses on the downside. And while I'm tempted to say that predicting market direction is an endeavor best suited for the financial analysts and mutual fund managers, I don't have much confidence in them either. This book is going to focus on sound investment strategies that are conservative in nature, provide positive long-term returns that keep pace with the market, or better yet, provide opportunities to do slightly better than the market.

But please, don't think that an approach based on conservative investment techniques has to be a slow path to riches. *It doesn't have to be.* The length of time it takes to build wealth is contingent on the investor, in terms of both how much they save and how well they invest. This book will teach you to earn a return, but there's no safe way to compensate for a lack of savings. You need to save every month and contribute to your portfolio. It would be foolish to throw your savings at overly risky investments in effort to prevent yourself from having to save more. The rewards simply won't be big enough, and the setbacks can be devastating. This is a very powerful concept to understand, because it puts the amount of success achieved entirely in the investor's hands. And while the investor cannot (and should not attempt to) predict market direction, the investor can control for their spending habits, how much they have left over each month to invest, and how wisely they structure their investments. Success is the result of small actions repeated every day for an extended period of time. So save a little extra and invest a little more. This is the most important ingredient to accumulating wealth through investments.

A good investment strategy should focus on controlling for the things over which we can actually exert control, and positioning ourselves appropriately when it comes to the things over which we have little to no control. We can't predict which companies are going to cut their dividends, so we are not going to build a strategy that relies on a specific company continuing to pay their dividends. It would be equally foolish to implement a strategy based on how many times we think the fed funds rate will be increased or decreased in the coming year. There is no reliable way to consistently predict things of this nature. And while trends do form, it's difficult to predict when they will change. We can make an educated guess, but we will never predict market direction with absolute certainty, so our investment strategy should not rely on our ability to make such predictions. We can, however, control for the amount of diversification we maintain, and we can similarly control for the types of assets that we feel comfortable investing in. So that's what we'll do. We're simply going to control for the things over which we have control, and we're going to position ourselves appropriately to protect our portfolios against the things that we cannot control.

If you're new to investing then you have an even bigger opportunity to do some learning along the way. My goal is to explain the world of dividend investing in such a way that the learning curve feels small, as this will allow both the new and the experienced investor to appreciate just how easy it is to implement a sound long-term investment strategy.

Chapter 1

Why Dividend Stocks?

The dividend is not what it used to be. Yes, it's still a distribution that the company makes after earnings are recorded. And yes, the company still isn't required to make a dividend distribution. It's still subject to double taxation (we'll discuss that sad and unfortunate conundrum when we get to the tax section). And, all else being equal, it's still better to receive a dividend than to not receive a dividend. But the dividend distribution is no longer the cornerstone of investing in stocks, and in my humble opinion, it should be.

Right now 84% of the companies that comprise the S&P 500 pay a dividend, and since 1926 approximately 45% of the total returns provided by the S&P 500 are attributed to dividends. What has changed is investor sentiment. Where the safety and predictability of a dividend paying blue chip was once in favor, many investor are now turning to growth stocks in search of large capital gains. The trend started in the 1990s, persisted right up until the tech bubble burst, and has since moved in and out of favor depending on investor sentiment and their appetite for risk. At the same time, many companies don't pay as high a dividend as they once did.

Prior to 1990 it was difficult to find a time when the stocks that comprise the S&P 500 paid distributions that collectively yielded less than 3%. There were brief moments when the yield dipped below this threshold, and those periods were indeed exceptionally brief. From the mid-70s through the mid-80s the yield fluctuated between 4% and 5.5%, and even from the late 1950s through the end of the 1960s it fluctuated between 3% and 3.5%. If we go back before 1957 the yields are even bigger, scarcely dipping below 4% and even exceeding 7% on a number of occasions. However, it should be noted that comparisons before 1957 are somewhat arbitrary because the S&P tracked only 90 stocks prior to this time.

From 1980 to 2002, the percent of S&P 500 companies that paid a dividend dropped from 94% to 74%. For those who continued paying dividends, the payout ratio dropped from an average of 50% to and average of 30%.

So why the smaller average yield today, and what does this mean for investors? The smaller average yield means one of three things, all depending on the stock. First, it could mean that the stock price has increased considerably. There is an inverse relationship between the price of a stock and its dividend yield. If the distribution remains stagnant and the stock price goes up, then its yield goes down, and vice-versa. This can happen during prolonged bull markets. But if there are enough earnings to substantiate an increase in stock price, then there's an argument that the dividend payment should also increase. Another explanation is that the company has a better use for the cash, and investing in a new project rather than paying a dividend will help the company grow. Lastly, it could mean that they're giving what used to be your dividend to senior management in the form of a large bonus. If it's the former, it may very well be good for the investor. The new project might pay off. But if it's the latter, shame on you for investing in the company, and shame on the shareholders as a collective group for allowing this to happen.

In reality, the shifting trend to lower dividend yields is probably a combination of the three. There are a lot of successful, highly innovative companies that are better off using their income to take on new projects. And if that's the case, then senior management probably feels entitled to their bonuses. If the stock keeps rising, the shareholders might feel the same way, at least until the stock becomes overbought and succumbs to a major price correction. At that point influential shareholders will bark, and someone's bound to lose their job. But a healthy and sustainable dividend keeps a company in check, and given that investors make buy and sell decisions that are at least partially based on how the yield compares to that of other companies, it helps the stock maintain a fair price. It's a detriment to the shareholder that dividend yield no longer holds the type of weight that it used to. But younger investors don't seem concerned. Companies like Facebook Inc. (FB) and Twitter Inc. (TWTR) don't pay any form of dividend, and these investments have achieved cult status among the millennial generation.

Take a look at Amazon.com Inc. (AMZN). On June 30, 2014, the stock closed at $337.49. Four years later on June 25, 2018, the stock closed at $1,699.80. Ringing in average gains of 125% per year for four straight years is indeed impressive, and though it's not every company that can do so, it is a perfect example of when not to pay a dividend. The company had a choice to make. They could either distribute their earnings to the shareholders in the form of a dividend or they could reinvest the earnings in new projects. And those new projects have been successful, so much so that the shareholders were better off not receiving a dividend.

Amazon.com Inc. (AMZN) started out in 1995 as an online bookseller, and its beginnings were so small that the very first book sold shipped directly from Jeff Bezos' garage. Since then the company has expanded into a "*near*" monopoly in the online one-stop shopping experience. As everyone knows, they'll sell you just about anything. The company clearly has had better uses for its cash than distributing it to shareholders, and this has been illustrated in both projects and acquisitions. It made more sense to develop the Kindle than to distribute a dividend, because the Kindle has been highly successful and has revolutionized how we read. It also brought in a lot of revenue, which is of critical importance. Similarly, it made more sense to acquire CustomFlix and turn it into CreateSpace.com than to distribute a dividend, because the project was again both successful and revolutionary. The truly brilliant thing about these acquisitions is that they allow the company to generate revenue without having to invest so much as a penny in inventory. They've done this sort of thing over and over and over again, making smart acquisitions at the cost of distributing a dividend, with their 2017 purchase of Whole Foods Market being one of the most significant. When a company grows at this pace, it makes sense to reinvest its cash internally rather than paying a dividend. A stock is never going to yield a 125% dividend. But when capital appreciation reaches this level, paying a dividend in line with other companies in the S&P 500 is arbitrary. So long as the company continues to grow and churn out profits, the shareholder is better off holding the growth stock than they are buying into a blue chip that will yield a percent or two.

There's just one caveat. A stock like Amazon.com Inc. (AMZN) is going to attract attention, which in turn will attract an ever-growing population of speculators, which creates the potential for the stock price to reach unsustainable levels. At the time of writing, Amazon.com Inc. (AMZN) has a P/E ratio of 79 (when we get to *Chapter 6: Attributes to Consider When Selecting Stocks* we'll see that a ratio around 12 is ideal, and a market average of even 30 is historically high and considered dangerous). What this basically means is that if Amazon.com Inc. (AMZN) were to maintain the exact same earnings that they currently have, it would take them 79 years to earn the amount of money that shareholders are currently paying for the stock.

I'm not going to make projections on what will happen to Amazon.com Inc. (AMZN). A company is not the same as its stock. They are two completely separate entities. And while a stock may be a good buy or an expensive buy at any given time, its price is the result of investor behavior. A company can be run exceptionally well and earn profits year after year, but if the stock is selling for more than it's worth purely as a result of strong investor sentiment, the price is eventually going to succumb to a correction. At the same time, while Amazon.com Inc. (AMZN) has been successful with its acquisitions and has increased its bottom line, there has never been a company in history capable of maintaining this rate of growth indefinitely. The fact that there's an antitrust concern seems to be ignored in the current pricing of the stock. Some investors are speculating that the company might be broken up like a monopoly. But most aren't worried. Even if a major correction is on the horizon, a stock can continue to increase in value for years before the correction occurs. It's all contingent on investor sentiment and behavior. Simply identifying a stock that appears overpriced is very different from predicting when the correction will take place, and as I explained in the introduction, we are not going to implement investment strategies based on our ability to predict events. Rather, we're going to implement strategies based on the elements that we can control, such as how much we save, the asset classes we invest in, and our willingness to reinvest dividends through both "good" and "bad" markets.

A stock trading at a P/E ratio of 79 strikes me as extremely risky. But it also looked risky in June of 2014 when it sold for $337.49. Earnings were smaller, and it had a P/E ratio of approximately 600, yet the upside potential has been huge. There are investors who have made a lot of money off of Amazon.com Inc. (AMZN) because they were willing to assume the risk. But there could be a news release at any moment that will prompt those same investors to abandon the stock. The strategies we're going to discuss are much more conservative than trying to predict when a stock will fall from grace.

The solution to any type of risk, of course, is diversification. And by diversification I don't mean that you should go out and find two dozen different stocks capable of reaching P/E ratios above 70. Such a tactic does nothing more than increase the probability that you're holding not just one, but many toxic stocks in your portfolio. Rather, you should invest broadly in a variety of markets, to the extent that no single security can make or break your portfolio. Yes, Amazon.com Inc. (AMZN) has made a lot of people rich. But when they bought the stock there was no guarantee that it would keep going up. And with a price that now exceeds $1,500 per share, there's no guarantee that it's a safe place to park your money.

Diversifying to the point that your exposure to Amazon.com Inc. (AMZN) will have a small impact on your portfolio is one method to control for risk. Granted, a properly diversified portfolio would have only a hint of exposure to the huge upside gains that Amazon.com Inc. (AMZN) has garnered, but it also protects the portfolio from the harsh downside risk that could be lurking in the shadows. This is where the dividend paying stocks gain importance.

In the following chapter we'll not only discuss the importance of added income, but from a mathematical standpoint we'll see how compounding, or the practice of always reinvesting your dividends, creates exponential returns over time. Dividend investing is about more than just building a stream of income that can be spent; the dividend is also a tool that will help us accumulate more holdings. And that's where the importance of a good dividend comes into play. Certainly, we have our work cut out, because stocks, as measured by the S&P 500, don't yield what they used to. And just a 1% reduction in dividend income can equate to hundreds of thousands of dollars in foregone appreciation over the long-haul. The strategies we discuss are going to incorporate large holdings in a variety of index funds, like the S&P 500 (SPY), and we'll look for other ways to get our portfolio yield up above what the S&P 500 has historically provided. Over time we expect to build a larger portfolio because of the added effort.

Chapter 2

Compound Interest

The most important concept of investing is the time value of money. And it's very easy to understand. A dollar invested today is worth more than that same dollar invested ten years from today, because if you wait to invest then you miss out on all those years of returns. This is the reason why we're all encouraged to start saving for retirement at such a young age. And it's also the reason why we have to pay interest whenever we borrow money. If you took Finance 101 in college they probably had you set up an amortization table to forecast the return on an investment. Or they gave you a formula that accomplishes the same end without the burden of formatting a spreadsheet.

It's important to understand that there's a difference between interest that compounds for us and interest that compounds against us. When we invest in stocks, receive dividends, and then reinvest the dividends, the interest is compounding for us, and over time our returns are multiplied. Say we have $5,000 invested in a stock that yields 3%. Over the course of a year we'll receive dividend income of $150. If we reinvest the $150 it brings our total holdings up to $5,150. Now the 3% yield is applied to $5,150 in holdings rather than just the initial $5,000. Throughout the second year we'll receive dividend income of $154.50. So by reinvesting our dividends we received an extra $4.50. This might seem small, but that's okay. We've just started to compound and this is a long-term strategy. In real life that stock price will change (hopefully for the better) as well as the dividend payment (again, we hope for the better). But let's ignore this impact and focus just on compounding. If the price and dividend yield remains constant, at the end of 10 years our investment will be worth $6,719.58 and will provide annual dividend income $201.59. After 20 years our investment will be worth $9,030.56 and will provide annual dividend income of $270.92. After 30 years the investment will reach $12,136.31 and pay an annual dividend of $364.09.

In real life there are other variables to consider. The company might cut its dividend. It might stay the same. Or it might raise the dividend every single year. The price of the stock will fluctuate, and also succumb to long-term trends. Maybe it will trend down. Maybe it will trend up. In order to make an investment in the stock, we should have some confidence that both the price and dividend payment will increase. This won't always happen. But if we invest in a portfolio of carefully selected dividend payers, we can expect to receive, on average, capital gains and larger dividends that make the results even better than what is illustrated above. The same concept applies to bonds and real-estate, given that interest and rents compound the same way if reinvested.

It's nice to be on the receiving end of an interest payment. But that's not always the case. When we borrow money to acquire a possession, the interest works against us, and over time the amount we have to pay is also multiplied. Credit card debt is the most prevalent example of interest compounding against the borrower. At the time of writing the average credit-card-carrying American is holding debt of $5,839, meaning, of course, that some people carry no debt while others carry significantly more. And those carrying debt are holding it month after month, perhaps chipping away at it over time, or maybe allowing it to grow even more out of control. But anyone who carries a balance isn't just paying interest on the price of their purchases; they're also paying interest on the balance that exists at the end of each month. In other words, they pay interest on whatever interest they haven't paid yet. And this allows the debt to keep getting bigger and bigger.

Debt isn't necessarily bad, but with credit card debt it almost always is. There's a huge difference between taking on debt to acquire a consumable item, like just about every credit card purchase, and taking on debt to acquire an asset that will appreciate in value, such as a home. Yes, the interest on your mortgage will compound against you, but you're also buying your home with hopes that it will appreciate in value.

When you first take out a mortgage the overwhelming majority of each payment goes towards interest and just a small portion goes towards reducing the principal. Over time, the principal will get smaller and smaller, and the result is that each payment is then composed of less interest and more principal. The faster you pay off the principal, the less interest you pay over the life of the loan. In this circumstance I'm going to say that the homebuyer benefits from taking out a loan for two important reasons. One, it's possible that the home will increase in value by more than the amount of interest paid, so in this regard the buyer has incurred the interest expense in order to acquire an assets that will return more than the cost of the house and interest combined. And two, one of the benefits of buying a home is the free rent that goes along with it. You don't have to write a check to your landlord each month, and assuming the home appreciates in value, you get your money back when you sell it. The mortgage payment is very different than rent in that it is likely to provide a return later in life.

Another common debt purchase is your car. And though most of us need transportation just as badly as we need a place to live, in this case the interest truly works against you. Unless the car is a collectable, it's only going to depreciate in value. This doesn't mean that everyone who drives a car has the power of compound interest working against them. It takes some discipline, but one of the best things you can do for your budget is to drive the same car for as long as it gives good performance. It's almost as powerful as the financial freedom that comes with owning your home. Making your very last car payment is a wonderful feeling, but having your car finally paid off doesn't mean it's time to start shopping for the newest model. Keep driving the one you have for as long as it handles well and doesn't require a host of expensive (*and time consuming*) repairs. The real challenge pertains to what you do with your money once the car is finally paid off. My advice is to continue making car payments to yourself and hold them in an interest bearing account. You've already grown accustomed to making a monthly payment, so you should be able to set the money aside without cutting back elsewhere. Let the money add up and earn interest. Then, when it really is time to go shopping for a new car, you should have accumulated far more than the required down payment, if not enough to simply buy the car outright. That's where you should strive to be. And once you get there, continue to make monthly payments to yourself so that you can do the same with your next car, and then the car after that. With this approach, you'll earn interest as you finance your next car rather than pay interest as you finance an existing car.

The successful dividend investor does so much more than just buy dividend stocks; they make sure that they're playing for the right team. It's all about earning interest rather than paying interest, and if you structure your finances appropriately, then a mixture of interest, dividends, and rents should work for you instead of against you.

Compound interest is indeed a powerful tool when it comes to wealth accumulation. Albert Einstein once said, "Compound interest is the eighth wonder of the world. He who understands it, earns it ... he who doesn't ... pays it." These words are very true. Success in any endeavor isn't a single action. It's a series of smart decisions that you have to keep making over and over again in order to build your success. If you want to be successful in building wealth by investing in dividend-paying assets, you have to reinvest the dividends.

To illustrate this *eighth wonder of the world* lets compare an investment made by an investor who doesn't bother to reinvest the dividends to one who does. This time we'll include the capital appreciation, and we'll assume that the companies increase their dividends in conjunction with their earnings. This means that the dividend yield remains constant, because the payment increases along with the value of the stock. In real life it won't happen exactly like this, but many companies strive to increase their dividend on an annual basis, so our assumption is not too far off. For those of you who did take Finance 101 in college, these tables should look familiar.

Consider an investor who contributes $6,000 per year to his portfolio; he expects to earn annual capital gains of 7.75%, a dividend yield of 3.50%, and he is going to reinvest the dividends. At the end of ten years he will have contributed $60,000 and his portfolio will be worth $112,972, for a total gain of $52,972. He will also have annual dividend income of $3,954. Even if he stops making contributions to the portfolio at this time, he can expect the dividends to increase annually during sound economic periods. In the table it shows dividend income of $3,554 for the last year computed. But moving forward the dividend yield of 3.50% will be applied to the ending balance of $112,972, which is where the amount of $3,954 comes from.

Year	Beginning Balance	Contribution	Rate of Return	Capital Gain	Dividend Yield	Dividends	Ending Balance
2020	-	6,000	7.75%	465	3.50%	210	6,675
2021	6,675	6,000	7.75%	982	3.50%	444	14,101
2022	14,101	6,000	7.75%	1,558	3.50%	704	22,362
2023	22,362	6,000	7.75%	2,198	3.50%	993	31,553
2024	31,553	6,000	7.75%	2,910	3.50%	1,314	41,778
2025	41,778	6,000	7.75%	3,703	3.50%	1,672	53,153
2026	53,153	6,000	7.75%	4,584	3.50%	2,070	65,807
2027	65,807	6,000	7.75%	5,565	3.50%	2,513	79,886
2028	79,886	6,000	7.75%	6,656	3.50%	3,006	95,548
2029	95,548	6,000	7.75%	7,870	3.50%	3,554	112,972

If we assume the same return but the investor does not reinvest the dividends, his portfolio will perform as follows:

Year	Beginning Balance	Contribution	Rate of Return	Capital Gain	Ending Balance		Dividend Yield	Dividends
2020	-	6,000	7.75%	465	6,465		3.25%	210
2021	6,465	6,000	7.75%	966	13,431		3.25%	405
2022	13,431	6,000	7.75%	1,506	20,937		3.25%	632
2023	20,937	6,000	7.75%	2,088	29,025		3.25%	875
2024	29,025	6,000	7.75%	2,714	37,739		3.25%	1,138
2025	37,739	6,000	7.75%	3,390	47,129		3.25%	1,422
2026	47,129	6,000	7.75%	4,117	57,246		3.25%	1,727
2027	57,246	6,000	7.75%	4,902	68,148		3.25%	2,056
2028	68,148	6,000	7.75%	5,746	79,894		3.25%	2,410
2029	79,894	6,000	7.75%	6,657	92,551		3.25%	2,792
							Total	**13,666**

At the end of ten years his investments will have grown to only $92,551 and he will have $13,666 in idle cash that was not reinvested, for a total value of $106,217. He's worse off by $6,755. But keep in mind that this is only a ten year span. The average retirement investor should be investing for 30 to 40 years, and over extended periods of time the difference will grow wider. Dividends compound in your favor. But if you don't reinvest them, it's as if the lost wealth compounds against you.

While it's easy to illustrate the value of reinvesting dividends versus not reinvesting dividends, it's more difficult to compare the difference between holding growth stocks to holding dividend stocks. By investing in dividends stocks we reap the power of compounding. But this doesn't mean that other investments, such as holding a non-dividend payer like Amazon.com Inc. (AMZN), won't outweigh the benefits of compounding. In other words, if it's possible to earn larger capital gains from holding growth stocks, might we be better off without the dividends? To an extent, *yes*. And to an extent, *no*. Our reliance on different investments, and the dividend yields that they offer, will change over time. And implementing a strategy that accounts for this change will be discussed in the coming chapters. But to provide a short and concise preview, it all comes down to proper diversification as we control for risk. It's important to understand that Amazon.com Inc. (AMZN) is an extreme example that is not representative of the return that can be expected from investing in a large pool of growth stocks. But do growth stocks as a whole perform better than dividend stocks? And if they do, why do we want to build a portfolio around dividend income? Let's take a look at both sides of the coin.

Those who advocate against dividend paying stocks will point to a company like Tesla Inc. (TSLA), who, like Amazon.com Inc. (AMZN), has achieved exponential growth without ever having paid a dividend. And proponents of dividend investing might point to Microsoft Corporation (MSFT), a company that first started paying dividends in 2003 and still managed to reinvest in new projects as its stock price pummeled the S&P 500. I'm not going to make an argument based on any handful of companies, because for every growth stock that achieves exponential returns, thus making the dividend paying stocks look inferior, there are many more growth stocks that failed and became worthless. And when we compare trends in stocks it's important to keep in mind that the results are often skewed due to a survivorship bias. Those that failed and went out of business, and resultantly never paid a dividend, don't get picked in long-term comparisons simply because their existence wasn't long-term.

A more meaningful comparison is to compare index funds, particularly those with a high dividend yield to those with a small dividend yield, and then determine whether or not the yields are large enough to account for the difference in capital appreciation. But first, let's make sure we all understand what an index fund is. An index is simply a group of holdings used to measure the performance of a market. An index of stocks would be used to measure the stock market, and an index of real estate investment trusts (REITs) would be used to measure the real estate market. The Dow Jones Industrial Average is a common index used to measure the performance of large cap stocks. It holds 30 different companies, and the combined performance of those companies is used to measure the health of the stock market. An index fund, as the name implies, is a fund that holds the same 30 stocks as the index. When we invest in this type of fund we aren't paying a large fee for a fund manager to select stocks that she thinks will outperform the greater market. Rather, we simply invest in the 30 stocks used to measure the market, and our performance thus mirrors that of the underlying index. The Dow Jones Industrial Average, of course, isn't the only index we could invest in. We could also purchase an index fund that tracks growth stocks, or an index fund that tracks dividend stocks. And for purposes of evaluating our investment in dividend paying stocks, we're going to compare the historical performance of a dividend index to the historical performance of a growth index.

Let's take a look at the Vanguard Growth ETF (VUG), which at the time of writing has a dividend yield of 1.07%. And let's also take a look at the iShares Select Dividend ETF (DVY), which at the time of writing yields 3.44%. And we'll compare both of these index funds to the SPDR Dow Jones Industrial Average ETF (DIA), which at the time of writing yields 1.95%.

It's important to note that even with the growth fund we get a little bit of dividend income. An investment in VUG still provides the benefit of compounding, but to a much smaller extent than that of our dividend fund, DVY. Even when it comes to growth stocks most indices will provide at least a tiny amount in the way of dividend income. But for now, let's ignore the impact of reinvesting dividends and compare the capital appreciation between the funds. Over a five year investment horizon ending 9/30/2018 we get the following returns:

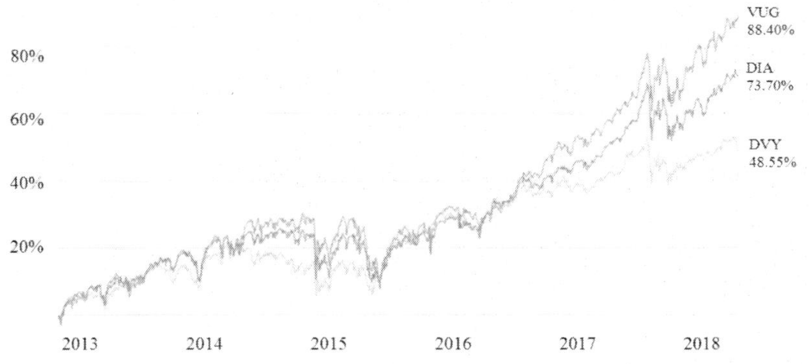

Vanguard Growth ETF (VUG): 88.84% capital appreciation over 5 years

SPDR Dow Jones Industrial Average ETF (DIA): 73.70% capital appreciation over 5 years iShares Select Dividend ETF (DVY): 48.55% capital appreciation over 5 years

While the 3.44% yield of the iShares Select Dividend ETF (DVY) is appealing, buying into a fund too concentrated around dividend payers didn't pay off during this five year interval. There's a 25.15% difference in appreciation between this fund and the SPDR Dow Jones Industrial Average ETF (DIA), yet the difference in dividend yield is only 1.49%. Even with the power of compounding on our side, we can't make up for a 25.15% difference in performance with an extra 1.49% in annual dividend yield. The same can be said of the Vanguard Growth ETF (VUG), which did 39.85% better than the iShares Select Dividend ETF (DVY) and 14.70% better than the SPDR Dow Jones Industrial Average ETF (DIA). The differences in capital appreciation are simply too big, and the dividend yields offered do not serve as a consolation. This doesn't mean that the power of compounding can't work to our advantage. It simply means that a big dividend yield isn't always in our best interest.

Those who start investing early in life are likely to have 30 to 40 year investment horizons. And five years is a very short interval in this context. There's no guarantee that growth funds will consistently outperform. But here it not only outperformed, *it outperformed by a lot*. Our goal is to build a well-diversified portfolio, and early in your investment career it's important to make room in the portfolio for growth, even at the expense of dividend yield. Growth funds can be used to increase the size of the portfolio, which in turn will increase the capital that is available to earn dividends in the future.

For the long-term investor, the 1.07% dividend yield offered by Vanguard Growth ETF (VUG) should not be ignored. For the sake of argument, let's say our investor decides to forgo a diversified portfolio and invest entirely in the growth fund. We'll assume the same $6,000 annual investment, but expect a higher average annual return, say 11.50%, and we still expect a dividend yield of 1.07%. But this time we're going to invest for a full 30 years. We estimate that our portfolio will be valued at $1,820,911 at the end of this horizon, but if we invested in a growth fund with the same capital appreciation but no dividend stream, that same portfolio would only grow to $1,465,789, a difference of $355,122. That extra 1.07% makes a huge difference, and later on in *Chapter 4: Our Weapons of Choice,* when we discuss the benefits of keeping fees low, we'll see the same thing. An extra percent or two, be it from dividend income or from keeping fees and commissions low, will have a dramatic affect on our portfolio over an extended period of time.

Year	Beginning Balance	Contribution	Rate of Return	Capital Gain	Dividend Yield	Dividends	Ending Balance
2020	-	6,000	11.50%	690	1.07%	64	6,754
2021	6,754	6,000	11.50%	1,467	1.07%	136	14,357
2022	14,357	6,000	11.50%	2,341	1.07%	218	22,916
2023	22,916	6,000	11.50%	3,325	1.07%	309	32,551
2024	32,551	6,000	11.50%	4,433	1.07%	412	43,397
2025	43,397	6,000	11.50%	5,681	1.07%	529	55,606
2026	55,606	6,000	11.50%	7,085	1.07%	659	69,350
2027	69,350	6,000	11.50%	8,665	1.07%	806	84,822
2028	84,822	6,000	11.50%	10,444	1.07%	972	102,238
2029	102,238	6,000	11.50%	12,447	1.07%	1,158	121,843
2030	121,843	6,000	11.50%	14,702	1.07%	1,368	143,913
2031	143,913	6,000	11.50%	17,240	1.07%	1,604	168,757
2032	168,757	6,000	11.50%	20,097	1.07%	1,870	196,724
2033	196,724	6,000	11.50%	23,313	1.07%	2,169	228,207
2034	228,207	6,000	11.50%	26,934	1.07%	2,506	263,647
2035	263,647	6,000	11.50%	31,009	1.07%	2,885	303,541
2036	303,541	6,000	11.50%	35,597	1.07%	3,312	348,451
2037	348,451	6,000	11.50%	40,762	1.07%	3,793	399,005
2038	399,005	6,000	11.50%	46,576	1.07%	4,334	455,914
2039	455,914	6,000	11.50%	53,120	1.07%	4,942	519,977
2040	519,977	6,000	11.50%	60,487	1.07%	5,628	592,092
2041	592,092	6,000	11.50%	68,781	1.07%	6,400	673,272
2042	673,272	6,000	11.50%	78,116	1.07%	7,268	764,657
2043	764,657	6,000	11.50%	88,626	1.07%	8,246	867,528
2044	867,528	6,000	11.50%	100,456	1.07%	9,347	983,331
2045	983,331	6,000	11.50%	113,773	1.07%	10,586	1,113,690
2046	1,113,690	6,000	11.50%	128,764	1.07%	11,981	1,260,435
2047	1,260,435	6,000	11.50%	145,640	1.07%	13,551	1,425,625
2048	1,425,625	6,000	11.50%	164,637	1.07%	15,318	1,611,581
2049	1,611,581	6,000	11.50%	186,022	1.07%	17,308	1,820,911

It's also interesting to compare the returns after 10 years to those in the earlier example. The growth portfolio is worth more, but the dividend income is smaller. This indicates that funds aimed at capital appreciation should be included in the portfolio early on when we're focused on increasing wealth. As we near retirement we should then switch our focus to protecting our wealth and earning larger dividends. We won't make the change all at once, and we won't ever invest in just one type of fund. Rather, we want to start out with a portfolio that is more heavily weighted towards growth. Over time, we will gradually shift the weight of the portfolio to rely more on bonds (for safety) and large cap blue chip stocks (for the dividend income). By getting a strong return on our growth funds, we build a larger portfolio and therefore have more funds to gradually shift over into our safer and higher yielding investments.

For those of you holding investments outside of a tax-deferred retirement account, an abrupt switch can have negative tax consequences that will eat away a good chunk of your wealth. In this case, there's an even larger incentive to make the switch gradually.

The 30 year example presented above provides a good picture of what we're trying to achieve over the long-haul. We want the portfolio to be as big as possible so that we can earn a larger stream of dividend income in retirement, and capital appreciation combined with compounded dividends is part of the method we'll use to get there. The other part, asset allocation, plays an important role in protecting our portfolio from a downturn, while simultaneously allowing us to automatically buy low and sell high without having to predict market direction. Again, our strategy is based only on the things that we can control, not on predictions of short-term movements. The rate of return that we've used for the capital appreciation portion of the portfolio is an expected average based on long-term historical trends. It could be different moving forward, but if we rely on broad exposure to markets that have a history of always beating inflation over the long-haul, it's reasonable to predict that success will be achieved. Our actual returns might differ, and the true rate of inflation cannot be predicted. But by selecting the markets we want to invest in based on long-term historical trends, we can proceed with confidence that over time our investments will get us where we need to be.

If we go further back in time and look at the same three funds over the five year period ended 12/31/2010, thereby including the great recession, we get very different results, yet the trend in terms of which fund performed better hasn't changed. Our growth fund took a plunge in 2008 and bounced back with a 23.36% return by the end of the period. The Dow Jones Industrial Average did the same but with only a 13.17% return. And our dividend fund ended the period with a loss of 16.06%.

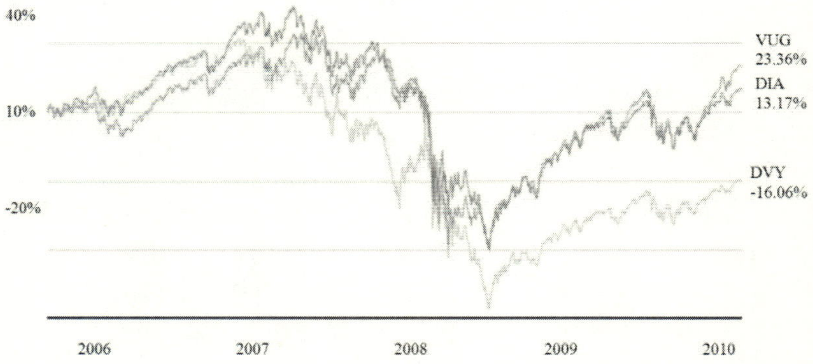

While these figures further suggest a preference for growth over dividends, it would be unwise to conclude that all we have to do is throw money into a growth fund, reinvest the dividends until retirement, and then switch over to the higher yielding dividend fund. This approach could potentially subject us to a huge capital gains tax depending on the type of account we're invested in. But more importantly, it should be understood that past performance is not always indicative of future performance. And while we want a dividend payer so that we can enjoy the power of compounding, when we start throwing value funds, small-cap funds, emerging market funds, and other asset classes into the mix, there's no guarantee that growth will be our best performer in the future, regardless of how it performed in the past. This is why we want to diversify. And while we're going to discuss diversification more thoroughly in *Chapter*

11: Asset Allocation, for now it's important to understand why the comparison we just made is meaningful.

All three of the funds we compared are equity funds, and they each exhibit some degree of positive correlation to the other funds. This means that although one fund performed better than the other two, they all moved in roughly the same direction at the same time, but to different extents. Looking at the chart, we see that as our growth fund took a big dip during the recession, the other two did the same. All three funds started to come back at the same time, though the dividend fund didn't make it back to positive territory by the end of 2010. This is what we mean by positive correlation. We'll discuss the concept more thoroughly in coming chapters. But for now we want to acknowledge that all three funds went up at the same time, and then similarly went down at the same time. This tells us that if we're going to diversify into different funds, we'll need to invest in more than just these three, because they are too closely correlated, and as a result won't provide adequate protection when the stock market tanks. Bonds serve as a safe haven when stocks perform poorly, and real estate can, but won't always, provide strong returns when stocks don't. When all three asset classes are combined our risk is reduced because the markets won't all move in the same direction at the same time, yet they all distribute a dividend in some form. These dividends will compound regardless of what the market is doing. And while a growth fund might provide just what it advertises—*growth*—we want protection during the periods when the growth fund (and any other equity funds we're invested in) depreciates in value.

Towards the end of our investing horizon we'll be more concerned with dividend yield than with capital appreciation. With time we'll progressively move in a direction where both safety and sustainability become more important than the long-term potential of a growth fund. Yet the benefits of compounding work in our favor at every stage in the investment horizon. The goal, again, is to grow the pie as a big as possible so that we earn as much dividend income as possible come retirement.

Chapter 3

Reinvest vs Spend

A decision that all dividend investors have to make is whether they want to reinvest or spend the dividends. In the above example there was $13,666 in cash that sat idle at the end of 10 years because the dividends weren't reinvested. This doesn't have to be the case. If the funds aren't intended for reinvestment, then the investor probably plans to spend them. This will, of course, reduce the value of the portfolio come retirement, but not all of your holdings need to be geared towards retirement. Some investors have holdings that are kept separate from their retirement accounts, all with the intention of spending the proceeds earlier in life. This is fine, so long as that's the purpose of the investment. But if you're holding the assets in a retirement account, then reinvesting is really your only option.

Investors under the age of 59 ½ pay a 10% penalty on early withdrawals. In addition, they are taxed on the withdrawal at their marginal tax rate, and we'll see later on that dividends paid into a non-deferred account receive preferential treatment. So if your goal is to actually spend the dividend income and forgo the benefits of compounding, you'll want to do so in a fully taxable account where the dividends will only be taxed at 15%. If your goal is to retire before age 59 ½, it's imperative that at least some of your investments are held outside of a tax-deferred retirement account.

The investor seeking an early retirement will benefit the most from reinvesting their dividends over their working years, all with the goal of building a stream of income to live off of until they can withdraw from their retirement accounts. Other investors might accumulate dividend income because they want to increase their standard of living, even during their working years. If your goal is to spend the dividend income as soon as it's earned you should still consider reinvesting at least a portion of the dividends. This allows you to reap some of the rewards of compounding, and doing so will then enable you to create an even larger pool of passive income from which to spend.

Regardless of your reason for spending some or all of your dividend income, it's important that you *only* spend the dividends, and nothing more. Even when an investment has appreciated in value we never want to eat into the principal because doing so will permanently reduce the dividend income that we earn for the rest of our lives. Yes, the investment may be doing well, but the number of shares did not increase, and dividends are paid per share. If you want to keep the dividend income flowing then you'll need to retain all of the shares. Spending the capital appreciation is a one-time indulgence. When it's gone, it's gone forever. But dividends are typically paid each quarter and, for just about any fund that pays a dividend, will continue indefinitely.

As we dig deeper into our strategy we'll see that there are times when we do want to sell shares, perhaps to invest in a different fund. Depending on how the funds are reinvested, such actions can either increase or decrease our dividend payments at that specific point in time. And that's fine. Rebalancing the portfolio periodically is a tactic used to control for risk. The impact on dividend income is temporary, and there will be a reversing impact down the line as our holdings move through their market cycles. But selling shares simply to spend the appreciation does nothing more than permanently reduce the dividend income, as well as the amount of invested capital.

The concepts discussed in *Dividend Investing* are aimed at the investor who wants to create an everlasting stream of wealth, rather than investing purely for an expense that they intend to incur at some predetermined point in the future. With this in mind, I'm going to repeat this rule because it's crucial to the success of a long-term investor—*it's okay to spend the dividend income if that's the purpose of the investment, but if you sell shares in order to spend the capital it will reduce the dividends you earn for the rest of your life.* Minus any number of unforeseen financial emergencies, it's much better to let your lifestyle gradually increase as you accumulate more dividend paying investments than it is to sell a portion of your holdings in order to partake in a one-time indulgence. This is a simple concept to grasp, but in practice it's an easy rule to break. It's up to you as an investor to exercise some self-control and stick to your strategy.

Chapter 4

Our Weapons of Choice

The Passively Managed ETF vs. The Actively Managed Mutual Fund

In the above examples we focused on both dividend income and capital gains in order to compare returns on the stock market. We also focused on index funds rather than individual stocks. And while the financial media provides extensive coverage on individual stocks, it's not necessary to invest in them. In fact, it's much easier to gain broad market exposure by investing in a fund (or more precisely, by investing in several funds).

Sure, individual stocks can be a lot of fun. And if you're enthusiastic about the work that goes along with selecting your own stocks, then it's perfectly fine to invest in them. I only caution that this should be done conservatively. Index funds provide greater safety. A company might take a hit and never come back. But when an index such as the S&P 500 gets pummeled, you can rest assured that it will eventually work its way back into the green.

When constructing a portfolio, our weapon of choice isn't going to be individual stocks, even if we have reason to believe that our selections *might* perform as well as Amazon.com Inc. (AMZN). Instead, we want to hold many, many stocks. There's safety in numbers. And while we do want to grow our portfolio, we want to do so in a manner that controls for risk. We want safety. And it's much more efficient to invest in a fund that provides the broad market exposure that we're after. So we'll be buying funds. And when it comes to investing in funds we essentially have two choices, the mutual fund and the ETF. We also have two different management styles to choose from, active and passive. And while there are notable differences between a mutual fund and an ETF, it's the difference between an actively managed fund and a passively managed fund that we're most concerned about.

The debate between actively managed funds and passively managed funds has been raging for some time, with academic studies favoring the passive approach, and active managers, of course, favoring the active approach. For our strategy it all comes down to maintaining low fees and reducing the impact of human error. I recommend only buying passively managed funds, and here's why:

When you buy into an actively managed fund you pay higher fees so that a fund manager and a team of analysts can be employed to research the market and select stocks that they believe will beat the market. The odds are stacked against them from the beginning, because not only do they have to beat the market, but in order to justify their high fees they have to beat the market by the amount charged. If an actively managed fund charges a full percent then they have to beat the market by a full percent. And they don't just have to do it this year. The fund needs to consistently beat the market by a full percent year after year after year. Of course, the law of averages comes into play, because there are literally thousands of actively managed funds and they can't all exhibit above average performance. These funds have so many assets under management that the culmination of their buying and selling forms the market average. By definition, they must succumb to the average. If half of the actively managed funds perform above average, it means that half don't. And when you add fees on top of it, most actively managed funds will provide below market returns.

Granted, each year there are plenty of funds that beat the market by more than the fees charged. And the financial media loves to provide coverage on these funds (at least while they're ahead). But beating the market one year doesn't increase the probability of doing it the next year. Each year is an isolated event. And when you narrow it down to the funds that did beat the average plus their fee two years in a row, the number gets smaller. Three years, and we have an even smaller number. *Four years, five years, six years?* I think you get my point. And when you consider that the strategies discussed in *Dividend Investing* are to be implemented over a 20, 30, or even 40 year period, the odds of achieving above average results with an actively managed fund are not good. The probability of receiving below average result, especially when you factor in fees, is actually in your favor. And the longer you hold the fund, the more likely you are to experience below average results.

It's interesting to note that academic studies show that when an actively managed fund beats the market, the chances that it will continue to do so actually decline. It's not because the assets selected one year have any sort of influence over the assets selected the next year. Rather, it's because of the behavior of the individual investors who buy these funds. There's a tendency for investors to rush into a fund that's doing well, just as there's a tendency for them to rush out of a fund that's not doing well. The more cash that investors throw at a fund, the greater the number of assets that a fund needs to invest in. There are only so many assets that will perform above average, so by increasing the assets that a fund has under management, its performance will be pulled closer to the market average. It's easier to find $10M worth of assets that will beat the market than it is to find $20M worth of assets that will beat the market. And the more money that investors throw at a winning mutual fund, the more winning investments the fund needs to find. So the larger a fund becomes, the more difficult it is for them to beat the market.

There are also tax consequences. When you own an actively managed fund your capital gains tax is not computed based solely on when you buy and sell the fund. It's also impacted by when the fund manager buys and sells stocks and other assets within the fund. The tax liability is then passed down to the fundholder at the end of the year, and depending on the fund it can be quite shocking. Actively managed funds do not subscribe to a buy-and-hold strategy. They are constantly getting in and out of the "right" stocks at the "right" time, and this not only drives up your taxes, but makes tax planning impractical. If you are inclined to invest in an actively managed fund, then by all means please hold it inside of a tax-deferred retirement account.

A passively managed fund is not only simpler, but better. Each fund is established to track an index. All the fund manager has to do is buy the same securities that comprise the index, and then reposition the fund whenever the index changes its constituents. The funds that were used above when we compared the performance of growth stocks (VGU) to dividend stocks (DVY) are perfect examples. And we compared both of these funds to one of the most commonly followed indexes, the Dow Jones Industrial Average (DIA). There are 30 stocks in the DOW, so buying into the DIA is the equivalent of buying those same 30 stocks. You don't have to worry about whether or not a fund manager and some group of analysts have the skills (*or luck*) to consistently beat the market. When holding this fund your results will mirror that of the market (minus a small fee), so there's nothing to worry about.

Yes, even a passively managed fund will charge a fee. The fund company isn't going to produce a product for free. But the fees charged on a passively managed fund are generally quite small. The SPDR Dow Jones Industrial Average ETF (DIA) currently charges 0.17%. And while we know that even small numbers can compound into big numbers, the fee here is so small that its impact is negligible. We saw in *Chapter 2: Compound Interest* that there is a benefit to compounding even the small 1.07% dividend yield that we might get on a growth fund. And we know that interest doesn't always compound for us, but can compound against us. That's what the fee on a fund is. It's the type of interest that compounds against us. Buying into a passively managed fund that charges a negligible fee will mitigate the impact of fees compounding against us, and will therefore leave more capital on the table that we can grow over time.

The difference between a mutual fund and an ETF isn't nearly as important as the difference between an actively managed fund and a passively managed fund, but the ETF is preferred. It's easier to trade in and out of, and the price is always known. A mutual fund does not provide the same ease and transparency, because it doesn't trade on a stock exchange. The value of a mutual fund is computed at the end of each day. So if you buy in during the day you don't know until the end of the day how many shares your investment bought. When you cash out during the day you don't know until after the markets close how much you'll receive for each share. Generally, you know what the markets are doing and you have some idea of what the transaction will be priced at. But if your goal is to switch from one fund to another, it will be a two day process.

An ETF, as the name implies, trades on an open exchange. The transaction is no different from when you buy or sell a share of stock. You know exactly what the price is at the time of your transaction. And when you sell shares the proceeds can be reinvested immediately. This is why I recommend the ETF over the mutual fund, and when we get to *Chapter 12: Rebalancing,* we'll see how important this is as we implement a rebalancing strategy.

It's not carved in stone, but most actively managed funds are set up as mutual funds, and most passively managed funds are set up as ETFs. I use the word *most* because some mutual funds track an index, just as some ETFs are actively managed. The real difference between the two pertains to how they're traded. But on average most mutual funds are actively managed and most ETFs are passively managed. It always pays to understand what you're buying before you buy it, and to be aware of the fees involved.

The strategy that we're going to implement focuses on earning dividend income by investing in ETFs that are passively managed. We want a fund that tracks an index for a small fee rather than one that attempts to beat the index and charges an exorbitant fee. This is the preferred way to invest in a fund, and it's much simpler than selecting individual stocks. As human beings we do more with our lives than track investments. We don't want to follow dozens of stocks, wade through all those financial statements, and listen in on countless earnings calls. We can simply purchase an ETF that ostensibly tracks the entire market. Or maybe we want broad exposure to a specific sector, or even a specific region. We can do that too. At the time of writing, funds that track the S&P 500 (SPY) yield about 1.73% and funds that track the DOW Jones Industrial Average (DIA) yield about 1.95%.

Those aren't huge yields, but they're acceptable, and investing in these funds not only provides broad market exposure, but allows the dividend investor to reap the benefits of compounding. My recommendation is to reinvest the dividends as soon as they're earned rather than waiting for what you hope will be a good entry point. This book isn't about market timing; it's about investing in markets with a history of providing strong returns over the long-haul. The investor who keeps waiting for the right entry point often finds that they missed the point entirely.

While current yields might be considered acceptable, most dividend investors aren't content with the yields offered by the S&P 500 (SPY) or the DOW Jones Industrial Average (DIA). These indexes aren't geared towards securities that pay strong, reliable dividends. There are other indexes to fulfill this purpose, and stronger yields can also be found as we branch into markets that pay interest and rents.

While the different approaches to constructing a portfolio are limitless, the point I want to instill is that index funds should constitute the bulk of your portfolio. They provide broad diversification, especially when you combine indexes from different markets that don't always react the same way in various economic environments. Think of your index funds as the nucleus of your portfolio. They ensure that the majority of your holdings keep pace with the market, and they do so for a very low fee. Savvy investors can then add individual stocks to the portfolio, but they should do so in conservative increments. If done right, modest exposure to individual stocks gives the investor an opportunity to gain an edge over the market in terms of both dividend yield and capital appreciation. It also gives them an opportunity to beat the market without incurring the management fees that accompany an actively managed fund.

When adding individual stocks to the portfolio, you are essentially taking on the role of an active manager. This is fine. But I recommend you do so with a conservative portion of the portfolio. We've already seen what small numbers can compound to over extended periods of time. So the goal is to take a small proportion of the portfolio, use it to select stocks that will outperform the market, and then allow those returns to compound year after year. You might decide to go after a stock that you expect to keep pace with the market if the yield is attractive. Or you might invest in a lower yielding stock that you think has potential for strong growth. By placing the bulk of your portfolio into index funds and then dedicating a small percentage of your capital to individual selections, you maintain safety while attempting to get an edge over the market. If successful, the benefits will compound in your favor. If unsuccessful, the damage will be contained, and the approach can be re-evaluated. There's nothing wrong with reverting back to a portfolio that's constructed 100% from index funds should your efforts to select individual stocks prove unsuccessful. And there's nothing wrong with forgoing individual stocks from the beginning and investing purely in index funds. The bulk of the material that we'll cover is geared towards managing a portfolio constructed from index funds. But first we're going to cover the art of stock picking. The next two chapters will quench the thirst of investors dedicated to making their own selections. The material will also lay a foundation for how the stock market operates and provide insight on the securities held by index funds.

Discount Broker vs. Full Service Broker

Our quest for a low fee investment strategy doesn't end with the decision to invest in passively managed index funds.

We have a second decision to make: do we use a discount broker or a full service broker? In the interest of keeping fees low, and therefore retaining more of our capital to grow throughout the years, I recommend the discount broker. In today's online environment, the cost of investing is incredibly affordable. But you have to select the right broker in order to reap the benefits.

Most discount brokers charge somewhere between $5 and $8 per transaction. That's how much you pay each time you buy into a fund, and you'll pay the same amount again when you sell the fund. We like that it's a flat fee. As you progress in your career and start contributing more to your portfolio, the cost per transaction won't increase along with the size of your contribution. If your discount broker charges $5 per trade and you invest $100 in a single fund, it will cost you $5, which is the equivalent of a 5% commission. However, if you invest $1,000 in a single fund, it still only costs $5, and this equates to a commission of only 0.5%.

The full service broker is at liberty to structure their fees according to their preferences (in other words, they're at liberty to structure the fee according to *their* best interest). Some will charge a periodic fee that's calculated as a percent of your portfolio. So if they charge 1% per year and your portfolio is worth $500,000, you'll pay $5,000 for their services, where someone with a portfolio valued at $750,000 would pay $7,500 for the same service. Yes, it's expensive. But if you decide to go with a full service broker, this type of fee structure is preferred. As the portfolio gets bigger, your broker's income increases. This aligns his interests directly with yours. In order for your broker to make more money, the value of the portfolio needs to increase.

Other full service brokers implement a commission based fee structure. It's very similar to the fees incurred with a discount broker, except that it's generally a percent rather than a flat fee, and this makes it a lot more expensive. It's not uncommon for a full service broker to charge a full percent per trade. So in our above example, the full service broker would probably tell you that $100 is too small a trade for them to execute. And once you're ready to invest something larger, say $1,000, they are going to charge $10 rather than $5. If you invest $2,000, it's going to cost you $20. As the size of your contributions grows, the commission correspondingly increases. But this isn't the only reason to avoid a full service broker who structures their commission as a percent of each trade. Their interests aren't aligned with yours. They don't earn more as your portfolio increases in value. They earn more as you trade more. This isn't good. Because trading in and out of stocks isn't guaranteed to boost performance, but it is guaranteed to increase your commissions.

Regardless of the fee structure implemented by the full service broker, their services cost money. The investor receives advice and guidance that isn't available through a discount broker. And for some investors, this is crucial to success. A good broker works the hardest during a bear market, because this is when customers need the most handholding. My goal isn't to paint a dirty picture of full service brokers. Like any profession, you'll find some who are extremely talented and highly ethical. And you'll find others who aren't. If you feel more comfortable working with an advisor, *Chapter 11: Asset Allocation* delves deeper into selecting the type of advisor who puts your best interest at the forefront. And that advisor is likely to recommend a strategy just like the one outlined in this book.

The goal of *Dividend Investing* is to forgo an advisor and implement a winning strategy on your own. We want to keep fees low and let our money work for us, not for an investment firm. Our weapons of choice are all low fee instruments. We like the passively managed index fund because it not only keeps pace with the market, but does so for a fee that's hardly noticeable. And we like the discount broker because the commission isn't just low, it's a flat commission that won't increase as the size of our transactions increase. When we purchase a passively managed index fund through a discount broker, we buy into the market at the lowest price possible. And we forgo "expert" advice in the process. The strategy that follows will illustrate why "expert" advice isn't necessary to succeed in the market. Once you've digested the strategy, if you feel that you'd be more comfortable working with an advisor, then by all means do so. But do yourself a favor and make sure you pick the right advisor.

Chapter 5

S&P 500 Dividend Aristocrats and the Use of Individual Stocks

If you're interested in picking your own stocks, the next two chapters are for you. We'll discuss the criterion to follow when selecting stocks as well as the attributes to consider before investing in a company. *It's going to be a lot of fun!* But first we're going to discuss the Dividend Aristocrats, which is an index of companies belonging to the S&P 500 that have increased their dividend every year for at least the past 25 years. To be a constituent, the company must also have market capitalization of at least $3 billion. It's a high bar to hurdle, and a relatively finite group of companies manage to find a home in the index.

Inclusion, of course, is not static. When a company meets the criterion they are added to the index, and when they no longer meet the criterion they are removed. There are roughly 50 companies in the index at any given time, but as a result of the 2007-2008 financial crises the index was temporarily reduced from 52 companies to just 43. It has since worked its way back up and currently holds 53 companies. But even during the worst of times the index has outperformed. Since it's inception in 2005 it has shown that over long investment spans it beats the S&P 500 while displaying lower volatility. This is, of course, attributable to the power of compounding.

What sets the S&P 500 Dividend Aristocrats apart from most other dividend indices, including the iShares Select Dividend ETF (DVY), is its focus on large cap stocks from different sectors. Most dividend indices rely heavily on financial, energy, telecommunication, and utility stocks. The S&P 500 Dividend Aristocrats is unique in that it includes stocks from all 11 sectors of the S&P 500. Many of these stocks won't yield as much as a utility stock. And that's fine. With the Dividend Aristocrats it's about playing the long game. A high yield right off the bat can be attractive, but sustainability and growth are more important. After you've held a stock for 10 years, the yield on its current price is no longer important. It's the yield on the initial price that you paid for the stock that matters. Assuming the stock has appreciated in value, a new investor is going to pay a higher price, and their yield on the stock will be lower than yours. The fact that the Dividend Aristocrats increase their dividend payments on an annual basis means that the yield on your initial investment will continually grow.

There should be room in your portfolio for high-yielding sectors like utilities, either as individual holdings or through an index fund. They are a wonderful source of income. But when you buy a lower-yielding Dividend Aristocrat, you're setting yourself up for the future. You're chasing after stocks that offer both a sustainable dividend and capital appreciation, and you want to see both of them rise simultaneously. There's added strength in holding companies that strive to maintain a reliable dividend.

When a company cuts or discontinues their dividend it has a two pronged effect. It reduces or eliminates the quarterly payout, and this causes downward pressure on the price. Prospective investors aren't going to pay as much per share after a dividend cut. Not only does the stock pay less, but reducing or eliminating the dividend is a sign from management that the company's outlook is changing. There's a small possibility that they need to keep the money in-house to invest in new projects that will increase the value of the company, but more likely than not, cutting or eliminating the dividend is a bearish sign that the earnings outlook is changing.

When a company increases its dividend the impact on price is just the opposite—it creates upward pressure. Each time the dividend is increased the yield goes up proportionately. The higher yield makes the stock more attractive, which increases demand and resultantly increases the price. This, of course, is by no means the only factor affecting price. Earnings per share is the most actively scrutinized measure. But virtually any attribute that a stock is measured by has at least some impact on the company's ability to keep raising its dividend. If earnings per share progressively decreases and never returns to what it once was, this will naturally force the company to either cut or eliminate the dividend. So when just the opposite happens, and the company routinely increases its dividend on an annual basis, it's an indication that other measures of the company are intact. The companies that comprise the Dividend Aristocrats have proven track records. And they don't want to tarnish that record by cutting their dividends during an economic pullback. Increasing dividends annually for a prolonged period of time isn't just good for the investor's cash flow; it's a sign of strength for the company.

An index fund that holds the S&P 500 Dividend Aristocrats (NOBL) is a fine addition to any portfolio. But when it comes to selecting individual stocks, this index is prime hunting ground for the dividend investor. By investing in the index we achieve market performance. Our holding will go up and down in conjunction to the index. We can then take measures to beat the index by adding a handful of carefully selected stocks to the portfolio.

If we assume a very simple portfolio, say 95% invested in the S&P 500 Dividend Aristocrats and 5% invested in individual stocks, there's a sense of safety in that the bulk of the portfolio will keep pace with the index. In the short-term we might see a loss, but as long-term investors we expect the portfolio to appreciate in value. With the 5% that we've allocated to our individual holdings we will go after stocks that either yield more than the index or that are expected to provide larger capital gains. Or it could be some combination of the two.

Picking the right stocks is important. It's easy to point out the Dividend Aristocrats after they've become Dividend Aristocrats. It's just as easy to say that you should have bought Johnson & Johnson (JNJ) ten years ago when its quarterly dividend was only $0.46 instead of the $0.90 that it pays in 2019. But when you first purchase a stock you have no idea whether or not the company will continue to increase its dividend on an annual basis. Not all of the Dividend Aristocrats stay in the index. Some of them cut their dividends, while others lose considerable market share. And while it's easy to say you won't include such companies in your portfolio, in practice this can be more challenging.

The dividend investor doesn't just need to develop a technique for recognizing a sustainable dividend, but must also learn the attributes that make for an attractive stock. If you posses the drive and motivation to research and follow your holdings, the benefits can be substantial. Success with individual selections is a combination of both skill and luck. The skill comes from understanding both the quantifiable attributes that make for a sound investment, as well as gauging future success based on trends for consumption and the company's ability to provide a superior product or service. Luck comes into play because any of your carefully selected stocks could turn out to be the next Enron. There's no denying that Enron had all the signs of a strong company, but they weren't. And that's where the dividend comes into play. A company's earnings can be manipulated, but dividends are real money. There is no fancy accounting trickery when it comes to distributing a dividend. A company can manipulate earnings, but they cannot manipulate a cash distribution. When a company increases their dividend every year for 25 years it means that they are generating real cash. The dividend investor should take note of this feat and consider the company for inclusion in their portfolio. Past success is not a guarantee of future success. But when you're selecting a stock from the Dividend Aristocrats you're selecting from companies that have achieved success, which is safer than selecting stocks from a pool of companies that are still struggling to acquire success. Whether or not the achieved success can be maintained is for the dividend investor to determine before they purchase the stock. It can be a fun game, but it's also a game that should be played in moderation.

There are many advantages to holding individual stocks in modest proportions. One of them is that the management fee is avoided. When you select your own stocks you essentially become the manager, and this not only provides freedom, but also savings. While the fee charged by an index fund should be small, it won't always be the case. If you diversify into a sector or region where the selection of available ETFs is limited, the management fee can be intrusive. Regardless of the size, management fees are typically deducted from the dividend payments and the investor might not even be aware of the fee if they haven't read the prospectus or checked the expense ratio.

With individual stocks the fee is avoided, which provides an advantage over funds that charge high fees. The commission paid to buy and sell a stock is generally the same as the commission paid on an ETF. So when it comes to fees and commissions it's only the management fee that makes a difference. If your stock selections lag the market, then having saved on the management fee is a moot point; you would have been better off buying into an index fund.

It's best to keep the number of holdings small. The greater your number of holdings, the more there is to keep up on. At the beginning you'll want to compare different stocks and pick the ones with the best attributes. Once this is done you'll need to continually monitor your stocks, keep up with their earnings, watch for news releases, and be informed of what's going on with the greater market. The more stocks you have to follow, the more time-consuming it becomes. That's one reason why it's best to use index funds to form the nucleus of your portfolio. It provides safety and diversification. From there it's okay to buy just one stock. Or maybe five. But keep the numbers small. Too many holdings can be bad for the portfolio. The goal is to get an edge on the market and make your portfolio perform better than the underlying index. If you pick a handful of winners then this will certainly be accomplished. But if you add too many stocks, then the performance of your holdings will conform to the average.

I recommend holding no more than five individual stocks at one time. Do your research and have confidence that they will be winners. If the S&P 500 Dividend Aristocrats is tracking 50 stocks, then holding 10 individual stocks moves your returns closer to that of the index. If you hold 20 individual stocks then your result will be even closer.

Your goal of selecting five winners is achievable. A small allocation also removes pressure from the process. The greater success of your portfolio will not be tied to your ability to pick stocks. Give your stocks room to breathe and don't let your emotions get in the way. Your success as a stock picker should not be evaluated based on how your stocks perform in the coming weeks, but rather how they perform in the coming years. With a conservative allocation there is no reason to second guess yourself and abruptly cash out. The decision to switch stocks should be based on a change in the earnings trend, the marketplace, political environment, or some other measurable event that leads to the rational decision to invest in a different company. Fear that you've made a bad decision should not be factored into the equation.

As stated above, if you implement this strategy and later determine that picking stocks is not for you, there's nothing wrong with changing your approach and relying 100% on index funds. Every investor has a different temperament and style. It's okay if your approach evolves along the way, so long as you keep the bulk of your portfolio protected throughout the process.

Chapter 6

Attributes to Consider When Selecting Stocks

Picking stocks is a skill that's honed over time. As investors develop this skill they conform to a style that matches their personality. Some prefer value while others prefer growth. Some subscribe to fundamental analysis and make investment decisions based on what they believe to be a company's intrinsic value. Others subscribe to technical analysis and make decisions based on analyzing charts. And while it's easy to apply labels to different styles, when you get down to it there are as many different variations to picking stocks as there are investors who pick them. The wealth of literature devoted to each of the different styles allows investors to learn from their predecessors and incorporate existing knowledge into their approach. We all have our own idiosyncrasies, and even when we subscribe to a specific school of thought we can still be influenced by other techniques. The dividend investor is only different from other investors in that we adopt our own take on what we consider a *safe* dividend. And *safety* is important because our goal is to hold our stocks for an extended period of time, all the while being prepared to move into a different stock should the forecast change.

Our goal isn't to invest in stocks simply because of a high dividend yield, but to invest in quality stocks that offer an attractive yet sustainable distribution. If the yield is both sustainable and exceeds that of the market, and the stock possesses other attributes that suggest good performance over a period of at least five years, then the stock should be a candidate for inclusion in the portfolio. With the right stocks we can increase the benefits of compounding without risking too much, if any, in terms of capital gains.

It's important to take your tolerance for risk into consideration when deciding how much, if any, of your portfolio should be invested in individual stocks. At the same time, your individual selections should not infringe on the amount invested in other markets, such as bonds and real estate. If, for example, your desired asset allocation is 50% stocks, 25% bonds, and 25% REITs, and you want to dedicate 5% of your portfolio to individual stocks, then you should reduce your investment in stock funds to 45%. This will give you a combined portfolio allocation of 50% stocks, and allow your bond and REIT allocations to remain at 25% apiece.

Stock picking is as much an art as it is a science. While covering every aspect of a stock that one could conceivably analyze is well beyond the scope of *Dividend Investing*, I'm going to present some basic attributes that every investor should consider before purchasing a stock, followed by a host of attributes that are particularly important to the dividend investor. Yes, we're going to dive into the financial statements, but don't think you need to be a CPA in order to read these statements. We're going to look at some high level attributes that every investor should be familiar with. And I firmly believe that reading footnote disclosures and understanding all of the subtle intricacies of earnings and valuation are not essential in order to feel comfortable with a company's financial position. If the company was able to trick their audit firm then they won't have much trouble tricking their investors. So you don't need to understand everything that the CPAs wade through when they audit the financial statements. A basic understanding of what the financial statements mean is sufficient. If you find financial statements intimidating, you shouldn't. We'll review them at a high level, and while deeper analysis is often beneficial, it's not crucial when it comes to picking a winning stock. I strongly believe that the most important attribute you can look for in a company is their competitive advantage. Is there something they are doing that can't easily be replicated? You won't get this from reading the financial statements. What you will get is a feeling for whether or not the stock is fairly priced given this competitive advantage. You'll also see that the indicators for a safe dividend are very straightforward.

There are plenty of resources available online that provide the basic attributes of a stock. *Yahoo! Finance* is a particularly popular site that is both free and easy to follow. They publish stock statistics that will save you the trouble of crunching numbers. This allows you to devote your time to analyzing the numbers rather than calculating them. They also publish full financial statements, and these generally include both the most recent year and two or three prior years. For the dedicated investor who wants to dive deeper, I recommend going to the company's website to download the annual 10-K reports, or you can search for the report at sec.gov.

If you're not familiar with the 10-K report, it's an annual report required by the U.S. Securities and Exchange Commission (SEC). Publicly traded companies are also required to file quarterly reports (10-Qs). These are public documents that hold the financial statements, and many of the statistics available on *Yahoo! Finance* are derived from these reports. The documents also provide very thorough explanations of the amounts reported in the financial statements. This is a great resource when further investigation is warranted.

Income Statement

The income statement can be used to analyze a company's revenues (or sales) and the expenses that are not only attributed directly to those sales, but the overall operations of the company. In general terms, it allows us to analyze how effectively the company generates sales, and how efficiently it manages expenses.

Provided here is a copy of the Apple Inc. (AAPL) income statement for their fiscal year ended 9/29/2018. You might find it helpful to refer back to this example as we review each section of the income statement.

Apple, Inc. (APPL)

Income Statement All numbers in thousands

Revenue	**9/29/2018**	**9/30/2017**	**9/24/2016**	**9/26/2015**
Total Revenue	265,595,000	229,234,000	215,639,000	233,715,000
Cost of Revenue	163,756,000	141,048,000	131,376,000	140,089,000
Gross Profit	**101,839,000**	**88,186,000**	**84,263,000**	**93,626,000**
Operating Expenses				
Research Development	14,236,000	11,581,000	10,045,000	8,067,000
Selling General and Administrative	16,705,000	15,261,000	14,194,000	14,329,000
Non Recurring	0	0	0	0
Others	0	0	0	0
Total Operating Expenses	194,697,000	167,890,000	155,615,000	162,485,000
Operating Income or Loss	**70,898,000**	**61,344,000**	**60,024,000**	**71,230,000**
Income from Continuing Operations				
Total Other Income/Expenses Net	2,005,000	2,745,000	1,348,000	1,285,000
Earnings Before Interest and Taxes	70,898,000	61,344,000	60,024,000	71,230,000
Interest Expense	-3,240,000	-2,323,000	-1,456,000	-733,000
Income Before Tax	72,903,000	64,089,000	61,372,000	72,515,000
Income Tax Expense	13,372,000	15,738,000	15,685,000	19,121,000
Minority Interest	0	0	0	0
Net Income From Continuing Operations	**59,531,000**	**48,351,000**	**45,687,000**	**53,394,000**
Non-recurring Events				
Discontinued Operations	0	0	0	0
Extraordinary Items	0	0	0	0
Effect Of Accounting Changes	0	0	0	0
Other Items	0	0	0	0
Net Income	**59,531,000**	**48,351,000**	**45,687,000**	**53,394,000**

Revenue - At the top of the Income Statement is revenue. Comparing revenue from the current year to prior years will provide an indication as to whether or not the company is growing. Ideally, we want to see revenue increase from one year to the next. Obviously, the bigger the year-over-year increase, the better. And any increase that scarcely keeps pace with inflation should not be considered an increase at all.

Revenue is a metrics for demand. It speaks directly to the amount of sales generated by the company. It does not tell us anything about how efficiently the company generated those sales. If revenue is decreasing and the company makes corresponding cuts to their expenses, the bottom line (net income) may very well increase. And while such a situation would actually increase profits (for the year) it's an indication that growth has stagnated. For a stock to be an attractive investment, we don't just want to see an increase to net income, but also want to see revenue increasing each year.

Cost of Revenue – While revenue alone is a good metric for measuring sales, it tells us nothing about how much those sales cost. What we also want to know is, *what kinds of expenses did the company incur in order to generate sales?* Cost of revenue speaks directly to the cost of manufacturing and delivering a product or service. It ignores costs that the company incurs irrespective of its output and focuses on labor costs, commissions, materials and supplies, and related overhead. It's a measure of costs that fluctuate with the level of output, which should increase as sales increase. A company with low cost of revenue as a percent of total revenue is thought to be in good financial position.

Gross Profit - Gross profit is a company's revenue minus its cost of revenue. It's beneficial to see this number increase along with the revenue, meaning that the company is not increasing costs by too much in order to generate additional sales. If sales are increasing, gross profit will tell us if the company was able to increase those sales by more or less than the corresponding increase in the cost of sales.

To compare gross profit between different companies, calculate as a ratio:

Gross Profit / Revenue = Gross Profit Margin

This type of comparison is most meaningful when made between companies in the same industry. The higher the margin in comparison to that of the company's competitors, the better.

Operating Expenses – Operating expenses includes necessary expenses to support the company's operations. Unlike the cost of revenue, these expenses won't fluctuate directly with output. Operating expenses include rent, research and development, the cost of equipment, administrative payroll, insurance, and a large host of expenses that a company incurs regardless of that quarter's production run. Generally, a company will attempt to reduce these costs as a means of staying efficient and competitive, or if the company is struggling, they'll reduce them just to stay alive. An increase in operating expenses could be an indication of coming improvements in the quality or innovation of their products or services. Or it could mean that they are slipping in terms of efficiency.

Income from Continuing Operations – This figure tells us if the company is profitable as a result of its primary income source. That is, *did net income go up because there is a demand for the company's product or service, or did they put themselves in the green by selling something extraneous like a piece of real estate?* It can also be referred to as income before interest and taxes. It is the culmination of everything we discussed above, but it excludes interest, taxes, extraordinary items, and other non-recurring events.

Companies acquire all sorts of assets in order to produce and market a product or service. And while they may eventually sell those assets at a profit (or loss), this income is outside the scope of their general operations and is not included in income from continuing operations. While such sales may affect a company's financial position, seeing continued improvement in a company's income from continuing operations is a sign of strength and stability. It means that they are growing as a result of their core business purpose, rather than having stumbled into an amazing one-time real estate deal. It's desirable that, on average, the bulk of a company's net income be derived from its continued operations, though unrelated gains are certainly welcome.

Like gross profit, we can also derive a ratio off of income from continuing operations in order to make comparisons between companies:

Income from Continuing Operations / Revenue = Operating Margin

Again, the higher the margin, the better. And the comparison is most meaningful when made between companies in the same industry.

Non-recurring Events – Sometimes a company looks really good in certain areas, yet for some reason it has negative net income for the year. Or maybe they underperformed in terms of sales, but net income still went up. In either case you'll want to take a look at the numbers booked under non-recurring events. These are one-time happenings that impact the bottom line. That amazing real estate deal alluded to above is a non-recurring event. It's also an example of the company making money. Another year there might be a natural disaster that destroys one of their plants. This, of course, would produce a loss.

If a non-recurring event leads to a loss you definitely want to dig deeper. It might be necessary to wade through the10K and review the footnote disclosures. But if it's a large company with heavy coverage, then a Google search might be an easier way to see what's going on. It could be a write-off of bad debt with no expected impact on future performance. Or it could be the result of litigation against the company, and depending on the nature of the litigation, there could be a residual affect that hurts their reputation and impacts future sales. If the company has discontinued operations it could explain why sales have fallen. But it could also be a sign that they're taking steps to improve efficiency. The numbers are just that— *numbers*. The interpretation is up to the investor. Reading financial statements in conjunction with articles published on the company often provides the needed insight. In this regard, larger companies with plenty of press coverage are much easier to evaluate.

A non-recurring event won't always influence your perception of the company, but if they have non-recurring events each year, and the losses are significant, it's a sign to stay away.

Net Income – Net income, often referred to as the bottom line, is basically sales (of all kinds, not just for the product or service that the company specializes in) less every expense incurred, from those required to produce or provide their product or service down to the cost of financing their operations and the interest and taxes they incurred in this endeavor.

While it's important to review the bottom line, an understanding of how the above pieces feed into net income is far more important. When reviewing a large number of companies it might be tempting to start with net income and move on to your next candidate if you don't see year-to-year improvement. I recommend starting with revenue instead. Look first for companies that have increased their revenue for at least three years straight, and don't waste any time with companies that haven't. If they pass this requirement, then keep reading and see if you're still interested by the time you've worked your way down to net income. If you are, then it's time to review the balance sheet.

Just as we did with gross profit and income from continuing operations, we can express net income as a percentage of revenue in order to make comparisons across companies:

Net Income / Revenue = Net Income Margin

As before, we're looking for a high ratio relative to that of the company's competitors.

Balance Sheet

While the income statement is our source of information for earnings, the balance sheet tells us about the company's overall financial position. *How many assets has the company accumulated? What kind of debt is it currently holding? And do assets exceed liabilities in order to provide a positive equity position?* These are the types of questions we'll be asking.

The entire balance sheet should be reviewed before making an investment. But different companies will show different types of assets and liabilities, especially if they compete in different industries. If one company manufactures a good while another provides a service, there will be items on their balance sheets that are not comparable. For this reason we are going to hone in on an assortment of key items that every investor should be familiar with.

We'll look at both assets and liabilities, knowing that in an accounting sense the true worth of the company is net assets, or assets held in excess of liabilities.

Assets – Liabilities = Owner's Equity

Owner's equity represents the value of the company, but this measurement is different from how the company is valued on a stock exchange. On an exchange the company is worth whatever the investors are willing to pay for it (or more specifically, what the most recent investor paid for it). The current selling price multiplied by the number of shares outstanding determines the market capitalization. But accountants aren't concerned with what investors are willing to pay for the company; they want to know the valuation of what the company owns less the obligations they've incurred but have yet to pay.

If we take owner's equity and divide by the number of shares outstanding, we get the book value per share. This, of course, will differ from what a share of stock sells for on an exchange. In most cases, market price per share will exceed the book value per share. And this is perfectly fine. Most value investors don't mind paying more than book value. Ben Graham, the father of value investing, advocated buying stocks with a price-to-book ratio of 1.5 or less, meaning he was only willing to pay 1.5 times the book price for a share of stock. Given this criterion, if we find a stock with a price-to-book ratio less than 1.5, or even less than 1, it should be a candidate for investment. Other attributes such as a solid profit margin or a strong outlook for growth are likely more important than book value. So when you find a stock with an attractive price-to-book ratio, consider it icing on the cake.

If you're unfamiliar with Ben Graham, you might want to become acquainted with his book, *The Intelligent Investor*. It's not geared towards building a portfolio around dividend paying index funds, but it's an excellent resource for any investor who likes to pick her own stocks. A lot has changed since it was first published in 1949, but it will forever hold its place as the foundation that value investing was built on. To this day, many investors consider it their primary handbook.

Provided below is copy of the Apple Inc. (AAPL) balance sheet as of 9/29/2018. It's important to note that the income statement provides earnings results over a period of time, usually a year. But the balance sheet displays the company's financial position as of a specific date. It doesn't report on all of Apple's fiscal year 2018, but rather shows what their position was on the very last day of their fiscal year.

Apple, Inc. (APPL)

Balance Sheet				All numbers in thousands
Period Ending	**9/29/2018**	**9/30/2017**	**9/24/2016**	**9/26/2015**
Current Assets				
Cash And Cash Equivalents	25,913,000	20,289,000	20,484,000	21,120,000
Short Term Investments	40,388,000	53,892,000	46,671,000	20,481,000
Net Receivables	48,995,000	35,673,000	29,299,000	30,343,000
Inventory	3,956,000	4,855,000	2,132,000	2,349,000
Other Current Assets	12,087,000	13,936,000	8,283,000	14,691,000
Total Current Assets	**131,339,000**	**128,645,000**	**106,869,000**	**89,378,000**
Long Term Investments	170,799,000	194,714,000	170,430,000	164,065,000
Property Plant and Equipment	41,304,000	33,783,000	27,010,000	22,471,000
Goodwill	0	0	5,414,000	5,116,000
Intangible Assets	0	0	3,206,000	3,893,000
Accumulated Amortization	0	0	0	0
Other Assets	22,283,000	18,177,000	8,757,000	5,422,000
Deferred Long Term Asset Charges	0	0	0	0
Total Assets	**365,725,000**	**375,319,000**	**321,686,000**	**290,345,000**
Current Liabilities				
Accounts Payable	55,888,000	44,242,000	37,294,000	35,490,000
Short/Current Long Term Debt	8,784,000	6,496,000	3,500,000	2,513,000
Other Current Liabilities	40,230,000	38,099,000	8,243,000	10,939,000
Total Current Liabilities	**116,866,000**	**100,814,000**	**79,006,000**	**80,610,000**
Long Term Debt	93,735,000	97,207,000	75,427,000	53,329,000
Other Liabilities	47,977,000	43,251,000	39,004,000	37,051,000
Deferred Long Term Liability Charges	0	0	0	0
Minority Interest	0	0	0	0
Negative Goodwill	0	0	0	0
Total Liabilities	**258,578,000**	**241,272,000**	**193,437,000**	**170,990,000**
Stockholders' Equity				
Misc. Stocks Options Warrants	0	0	0	0
Redeemable Preferred Stock	0	0	0	0
Preferred Stock	0	0	0	0
Common Stock	40,201,000	35,867,000	31,251,000	27,416,000
Retained Earnings	70,400,000	98,330,000	96,364,000	92,284,000
Treasury Stock	-3,454,000	-150,000	634,000	-345,000
Capital Surplus	-	-	-	-
Other Stockholder Equity	-3,454,000	-150,000	634,000	-345,000
Total Stockholder Equity	**107,147,000**	**134,047,000**	**128,249,000**	**119,355,000**

Current vs. Non-Current – You probably noticed that some of the assets and liabilities are designated as current, while others are simply included in the total. A current asset is a liquid asset that the company expects to convert to cash within the next year. An example would be all of the accounts receivable that the company expects to collect on within 12 months. A current liability is an obligation that will be paid in the coming year, such as accounts payable that will be remitted within 12 months under the normal course of business.

A comparison of current assets to current liabilities is important as we evaluate the company's ability to sustain current operations, where a review of non-current items, such as long-term debt, comes into play as we forecast on the company's value and ongoing profitability. The distinction is also important in terms of dividend payment, particularly as we forecast the company's ability to increase the payment on an annual basis.

ASSETS

Cash and Cash Equivalents – Cash is king. There's no way around it. Good sales and low expenses are important. It's the earnings per share that analysts most frequently make projections on, and it's the company's ability to beat those projections that send the stock higher. But not every sale is collectible, and if the company isn't bringing in cash it's going to catch up with them. As dividend investors we really want to know if there's enough cash to maintain the dividend during an economic downturn. If the company is heavily debt financed with very little cash reserves, it's a cause for concern. Creditors take precedence over shareholders when companies are liquidated. Even the lawyers get paid before the shareholders. But beyond the fear of liquidation, a low cash position means that the company could be forced to cut their dividend in order to pay back loans.

Some investors view too much cash as an indication that the company is not putting their capital to use effectively. As dividend investors this is a secondary concern. We want to buy financially stable companies, and a strong cash position is a good indication of stability. It keeps our dividends safe through both the ups and the downs.

In addition to cash as reported on the balance sheet, it also pays to take a look at the statement of cash flow. This statement shows all cash activity, and basically reconciles the change in cash position from one year's balance sheet to the next. If income from continuing operations is increasing, you want to make sure that cash flow from operating activities is also increasing. This won't happen in exact proportions. Sometimes a sale made this year won't be collected on until next year. But over time you want to see a smoothing out that brings these numbers together.

Accounts Receivable – This is what the company is owed due to sales generated in the normal course of business. Changes to accounts receivable can tell us a number of things about the company. If it increases with time it could be the result of increased sales. Similarly, if it decreases with time it could be an indication that sales have declined. By reviewing accounts receivable in conjunction with revenue it's easy to gauge whether or not it is increasing or decreasing proportionately to changes in sales. If it's not, further evaluation is necessary.

There's also the possibility that the company is just getting better or worse at collecting on their accounts. Or perhaps they've expanded into a new territory or marketplace that comes with different challenges. There's no hard and fast rule with accounts receivable. It needs to be reviewed in terms of what the company is doing. But if it increases or decreases dramatically without a corresponding trend in sales, it's a cause for further investigation.

A common ratio used to compare accounts receivable between companies in the same industry is accounts receivable turnover:

Revenue / Accounts Receivable = Accounts Receivable Turnover

To express as a factor of days:

365 / Accounts Receivable Turnover = Accounts Receivable Turnover expressed in days

This is a ratio that we want to be as low as possible, as a low ratio indicates timely collections.

Inventory – With inventory we really want to analyze trends. *How does it change over time?* And do the changes make sense based on whether or not the company is growing? When sales go down we should expect an immediate increase in inventory. But after this has happened we want to know if the company adjusted their production accordingly. If inventory keeps rising it's a sign of poor management. At the same time, *is a sudden boost to net income the result of increased sales or is the company depleting inventory from prior periods?* This all ties in to how efficiently the company is run, and a company that keeps tight controls on their inventory is desirable, not just because it costs money to produce inventory, but also because it costs money to store inventory.

A common ratio to compare inventory management between companies in the same industry is the inventory turnover ratio:

Cost of Revenue / Inventory = Inventory Turnover Ratio

The result represents the number of times that a company turns over their inventory throughout the year. The more it turns over, the better.

Property, Plant, and Equipment – PP&E is just what the name implies. These are the large assets necessary to conduct business. Land has the potential to appreciate in value, and therefore is reported at current market value. All other PP&E is initially reported at cost and then depreciated over time. When evaluating stocks where the book value is less than market value, PP&E is important because these are the big assets that will fetch the most in the event of liquidation. It means the company still has something of value should everything else go horribly wrong (though we won't be investing in a company if we have reason to believe that all else will go horribly wrong). Land and buildings could conceivably be sold for a gain over the purchase price, where most other PP&E will sell for a loss, but hopefully fetch something in the neighborhood of its depreciated value.

An increase to PP&E is often observed during times of expansion. Steady decreases to PPE&E will likely correspond to the company's depreciation schedule and should not be a cause for concern.

Goodwill – Not every asset on the balance sheet is a monetary or physical asset. Goodwill is more or less synonymous with brand recognition. Or more specially, brand recognition that was purchased from another company. When a company produces goodwill internally it does not appear on the balance sheet. The expenses incurred to build and market the business are, of course, recorded on the income statement. But no expense is directly tied to the brand recognition this produces, and therefore it does not get reported as goodwill. An exception exists when the company purchases another company and pays a price above what the company is valued at on their balance sheet. When this happens the premium paid is booked as goodwill. This treatment puts the investor at a disadvantage. It's difficult to do an apples-to-apples comparison when one company is permitted to show at least some of their goodwill on the balance sheet and another is not. It can also be argued that when it comes to goodwill, too much is a bad thing. It's an indication that the company paid a premium for a name. And should the company ever be liquidated, there's nothing for them to actually sell. This is an asset that does not have a direct use. A good exercise is to compare companies as though they do not have any goodwill on the balance sheet. Simply subtract goodwill from owner's equity, do a comparison, and then ask yourself which company looks more attractive. This gets us closer to the apples-to-apples comparison that we're after.

Intangible Assets – Goodwill isn't the only intangible asset on the balance sheet. The others will be appropriately grouped together as intangible assets. Companies often own patents, trademarks, and copyrights, and these intangible assets have value. Unlike goodwill, a company can sell a copyright. But that doesn't mean we don't encounter valuation problems with these assets. A company must report their patents, trademarks, and copyrights at cost, not at what they are truly worth. So just like goodwill, it's difficult to do an apples-to-apples comparison with intangible assets. I suggested above that you subtract goodwill from owner's equity for purposes of comparison. It's beneficial to do the same comparison with both goodwill and intangible assets excluded from owner's equity. This provides a figure that's referred to as net tangible assets.

LIABILITIES

Accounts Payable – Accounts payable is the complete opposite of accounts receivable. It's what the company owes for expenses incurred on a short-term line of credit. We know that it's desirable to accelerate the collection of accounts receivable, and there is always a concern that some accounts will not be collected. The same concern does not extend to accounts payable. So long as the company has the wherewithal to make good on their expenses, we'd rather they pay their bills as late as permissible per the vendor agreement. You can think of it as an interest free loan (albeit it very short one). By delaying their payments, a company basically obtains a cash float. The ultimate goal is to accelerate the collection of accounts receivable while postponing the remittance of accounts payable. A company that manages this well will have a financial advantage over a company that does not.

Just like accounts receivable, we can use a ratio to compare accounts payable turnover between companies in the same industry:

Cost of Revenue / Accounts Payable = Accounts Payable Turnover

To express as a factor of days:

365 / Accounts Payable Turnover = Accounts Payable Turnover expressed in Days

Where a low ratio is desired for the accounts receivable turnover, we want to delay our accounts payable, so a high ratio is desired.

Debt – The perception that debt is bad isn't always true. Just like personal debt, corporate debt can be used wisely, *though it can also be a cause for concern.* As we discussed above in *Chapter 2: Compound Interest*, there actually is good debt. When an individual takes out a loan for their education or to buy a house they are taking on debt that will pay them back. The house is expected to appreciate in value and it provides the homeowner with free rent for however long they live there. An education, while expensive, is intended to pay the individual back with a higher paying job. These are both great uses of debt. A credit card balance, on the other hand, does nothing more than compound interest against the individual. The same rules apply to corporate debt. There is good debt and there is bad debt. *Is the company issuing bonds to fund new projects that will pay them back in the future? Or are they taking out loans to keep themselves afloat in light of poor sales?* As dividend investors we are particularly concerned with debt. If the amount is small, then there's really nothing left for the investor to consider. But large debt holdings should prompt further investigation to obtain a better understanding of what the debt is for.

It's a great sign when debt levels are falling. Debt for new projects can be good, but it's still better to see debt going down and not up. It's an indication that previous projects are paying off. When reviewing companies from the same industry a comparison of debt as a percent of either cash or of total assets can be beneficial. It's also beneficial to compare debt as a percent of total equity. If two companies are comparable on other grounds, the company with the least amount of debt is preferred.

To evaluate as a ratio, compute as follows:

Debt / Equity = Debt-to-Equity Ratio

A low ratio is desired. But keep in mind there are many good uses of debt. In order to compare ratios under the proper context, an understanding of how the debt is used should be obtained.

EQUITY

In simple terms, equity is the book value of the company. It is the assets minus the liabilities, which equates to the net assets that remain and belong to the shareholders. If it's negative, it's a cause for concern. It means the company owes more than they have.

Different methods can be used to calculate book value depending on the different classes of equity reported on the balance sheet. For our purposes we will look at two of them:

Assets – Liabilities = Book Value (owner's equity)

(Assets – Goodwill – Intangible Assets) – Liabilities = Book Value (owner's equity)

We've already discussed how book value will differ from market value, and that a stock with book value greater than market value should be a candidate for investment. The second approach, which focuses on tangible equity, is also important. Goodwill will become worthless during liquidation. Patents, trademarks, and copyrights could, in reality, fetch much less than their book value in the event that they can even be sold. The very fact that the company is being liquidated indicates a lack of profitable earnings, which implies that their patents, trademarks, and copyrights no longer hold value. If the company is thriving, it's a greater indication that their intangible assets hold value and could be sold at a profit. But such companies generally don't go through the liquidation process.

Book value derived from net tangible assets provides a clearer, more conservative view of what the shareholder is likely to receive during liquidation. For this reason, it's the figure we'll use to compare market value to book value.

A common ratio used to evaluate companies in the same industry is the return on equity:

Net Income / Equity = Return on Equity

The higher the ratio, the better the company is thought to be putting its equity to use.

Retained Earnings – Retained earnings is part of equity. It is the sum of all net incomes that the company earns, less any dividends that it pays.

As dividend investors it's important to know that dividends are not an expense to the company. They do not get reported on the income statement and they do not reduce net income. Dividends are what gets distributed to shareholders after net income has been calculated. And while they don't increase expenses, they are a cash outlay and therefore have an impact on the balance sheet. A cash dividend will decrease retained earnings. It also reduces the company's cash position.

In order for a company to pay its dividend they must have both positive retained earnings and the appropriate amount of cash. It's important to understand that a net loss will decrease retained earnings, and thus impact the funds available to distribute in the form of a dividend. This is one reason why we want to invest in companies where net income increases each year. The other reason is that rising net income combined with increased revenues is a sign of both growth and efficiency.

While we do want to earn dividends, it makes sense that receiving them will affect the value of the company; *what once belonged to "the company" now belongs to us*. This is a tradeoff. But while a dividend payment will decrease retained earnings, positive net income will increase retained earnings. So what we really want is a company whose dividend distribution is less than its earnings, as this will sum to a positive impact on retained earnings.

As we work our way through the following attributes we'll see exactly how to identify the type of company we want to invest in.

Attributes

Reviewing a company's financial statements is the first step to determine if a stock is worthy of investment. If you don't like what you see on the financial statements then there's no reason to proceed further. It's time to move on to a different company and see if their stock fits your requirements. For companies that do show promise, in terms of increasing sales, managing efficiency, and maintaining a healthy balance sheet, there are further attributes that you'll want to review. Some of them pertain specifically to the stock. It's important to understand that a company and its stock are not one in the same. A company can have beautiful financial statements and the stock can still be overpriced. Sometimes it pays to bide your time and wait for a correction. Other times you're better off redirecting your efforts to a different company. While some of the attributes pertain solely to the stock, other attributes will incorporate figures from the financial statements, and thus pertain to both the stock and the company.

Volume – It's important to know the average number of shares that trade each day. This won't tell you if a stock is fairly priced or even a good buy, but it will tell you how liquid the investment is. Some stocks might only average a couple hundred trades each day while others average in the millions. Keep your eyes open because low-volume stocks are present in all segments, from large-cap stocks all the way down to microcap stocks. Low volume is an indication of a large bid-ask spread, meaning that to buy the stock you have to pay more than what the seller on the other end of the trade is willing to accept. The difference between the bid (selling price) and the ask (buying price) goes to the market-maker as a commission, and if the market-maker is willing to handle a low-volume security they are going to want a larger commission for their effort. You can think of the bid-ask spread as an additional fee that you pay on every investment, and the lower the volume traded, the more likely it is that you'll pay a higher fee.

If volume is too low it's an indication that you might have difficulty selling the stock once it's been purchased. If you own more than the average daily volume, or even a sizeable percent of the average daily volume, it will be difficult to unload the investment without driving down the price. So if you buy into a sock that only trades a couple hundred shares a day, watch it go up 15% and then try to sell it all at once, you'll probably drive the price down in the process and receive less than the 15% gain you were expecting. With some stocks you might not be able to sell them at all, at least not until a perspective buyer eventually pops up, and that buyer might not be willing to pay anything close to where the stock last traded. The same applies to ETFs. An ETF that tracks the S&P 500 is likely to experience high trading volume, where a junk bond fund could conceivably trade in smaller increments, have a higher bid-ask spread, and be more difficult to unload.

If your starting place for stock selections is the S&P 500 Dividend Aristocrats then volume should not be a concern. These are heavily traded companies that garner a lot of attention. But if you decide to stray into other areas, keep your eyes open and make sure there's plenty of trading volume before you buy in.

Trailing P/E Ratio – A big mistake that new investors make is thinking that the cost of a share indicates whether or not the investment is expensive. A stock that sells for $25 is not half as expensive as a stock that sells for $50, precisely because each company has a different number of shares outstanding. What you're really buying is an ownership interest in the company, and if each company has a different number of shares outstanding then comparing the cost of stock A to the cost of stock B is not an apples-to-apples comparison.

The P/E ratio is used to form some even ground. We might not be able to compare the cost of stock A to the cost of stock B in any meaningful way, but we can compare the earnings of each company in a way that is exceptionally meaningful. What the P/E ratio does is it takes the price of a stock and divides it by the earnings per share.

P/E Ratio = Price Per Share / Earnings Per Share

For example, if a company sells for $10 per share and its earnings is $0.75 per share, then it has a P/E ratio of 13.33. If the investor were to actually receive that $0.75 in earnings each year as a distribution, it would take the investor 13.33 years to earn back the $10 that she invested in the company

Generally speaking, the lower the P/E ratio the better. If the P/E ratio were to be 11 instead of 13.33, then it would only take 11 years to earn back the investment. The investor isn't going to actually receive the earnings, and if the company is paying a dividend we would hope that the dividend is less than earnings. If it's not then the dividend isn't sustainable. But the P/E ratio is still the most valuable tool we have for comparing the cost of one stock to another.

If the P/E ratio is high, it's an indication that investors are expecting higher earnings growth relative to companies with a lower P/E ratio. Otherwise they wouldn't pay the higher price. And while expectations of future growth might seem attractive, I'm going to warn against buying stocks with high P/E ratios because what this really means is that you're paying for future earnings that are only expected to be higher than present earnings; *they haven't materialized yet*. At the same time, if a P/E ratio is too low it's an indication that market sentiment is bearish. The shareholders wouldn't part with their investment at such a low price if the outlook was promising.

At the time of writing the S&P 500 has a collective P/E ratio of 31.32, and this ratio is considered high (and viewed by many as exceptionally dangerous). If we look at historical averages we see that the S&P 500 has a mean P/E ratio of 16.58 and a median P/E ratio of 15.68. These are considered much safer ratios, and a P/E ratio of 12 is considered attractive. The average P/E ratio will of course differ by sector, as some sectors are simply more expensive to invest in than others. The tech sector is a great example because there is potential for exponential growth based on some revolutionary new invention. Therefore, tech stocks on average have higher P/E ratios than the rest of the market.

When looking at the lower end of the spectrum, a P/E ratio down around 9 is thought to be dangerous, and anything below this is considered bearish and an indication of short selling.

It should also be noted that the trailing P/E ratio is the metric to focus on, as this ratio is based on historical earnings. They also publish a forward P/E ratio based on analyst estimates for future earnings. This ratio should be ignored due to the fact that the analysts are frequently wrong. The forward P/E ratio is both arbitrary and meaningless.

200-Day Moving Average – There's a saying amongst investors that asset prices will revert to the mean. This suggests that if the current selling price differs significantly from its historical average, the price will eventually move back in the direction of the historical average. A stock that has been moving up (or down) is expected to revert at some point. And while it cannot be guaranteed with certainty when this reversion will occur, it happens frequently enough that traders base their strategy on this attribute. Even though our focus is geared towards investing rather than trading, this attribute is still a valuable tool.

The 200-day moving average is a metric commonly used to measure a stock's current price in relation to its average price over the past 200 days. As the name implies, the average will change each day because it's a moving average, and this keeps the figure relevant. If a stock is priced too far above its 200-day moving average we assume that the price will eventually drop. If a stock is priced too far below its 200-day moving average we assume that the price will eventually rise. Our goal is not to make a quick profit off of this reversion. Rather, we're going to review a variety of attributes for each stock we consider. If we find a good candidate for a long-term investment, we'll buy it. But all else being equal, it's better to invest in a stock while it is priced below its 200-day moving average than to get in on a stock that's priced above its 200-day moving average. If two stocks are equally attractive, purchase the one that looks cheaper based on its current price in relation to its 200-day moving average.

Current Ratio – While our goal is to identify investments to hold for a minimum of five years, the current ratio is important in terms of analyzing a company's current sustainability. It is calculated as:

Current Assets / Current Liabilities = Current Ratio

A current ratio above one is an indication of stability, where a current ratio below one is a cause for concern. In other words you want the sum of the company's current assets to exceed the sum of the company's current liabilities. So long as current assets exceed current liabilities the company is in a good position to carry forward with daily operations. If the ratio falls below one then it's an indication that the company either needs to liquidate a long-term asset (which could disrupt future operations) or experience a disruption to its current operations. It's advisable to simply avoid investing in companies with a current ratio below one.

% Held by Insiders – To the extent possible, we want to invest in companies that are predominately owned by insiders. And if "predominately owned" is too ambitious, then we want insiders to at least own a sizeable holding in the company. *Why?* Because strong insider ownership aligns the interests of upper management with that of the shareholders. It prevents management from making decisions that improve their own financial wellbeing at the expense of the stock price. If they own shares in the company then every decision they make will be geared towards increasing the value of the stock. There are, however, plenty of successful companies with a small percent of insider ownership. Not every holding in your portfolio is going to have 20% of the stock resting in the palms of upper management. And while that's fine, it's still better to invest in companies with high insider ownership, especially if the percent of institutional ownership is low.

Typically, insiders are awarded shares by the company, and once the shares have vested they have the option of either holding or selling their stock. Some investors pay a lot of attention to actions of insiders. A good rule of thumb is that insider selling doesn't matter. Holding too much stock in the company you work for is poor diversification. If the company goes out of business then you lose both your job and your investment. From that perspective, it makes sense for an insider to sell their stock as soon as it vests and then reinvest the proceeds in a different company. At the same time, they could be selling their shares simply because they want to spend the money. Investment decisions should not be based on insider selling. There are too many variables to consider when it comes to why an insider might sell, and attempting to analyze trends in insider selling reveals absolutely nothing about the company. Conversely, when an insider makes the decision to buy the company stock (that is, they purchase shares with their own money in addition to those that they are awarded for their work) it's an incredibly bullish signal. It's a sign of extreme confidence when insiders want to hold more stock than what has been awarded to them by the company. When this situation arises, a conservative investment in the company, even when other attributes are less than ideal, is warranted.

% Held by Institutions – This attribute holds more importance than insider ownership. It can make or break your investment decision. It's the institutional investors who truly set the price of a stock, and they do this by buying and selling in large quantities. In *Chapter 4: Our Weapons of Choice* we discussed the pitfalls of investing in an actively managed fund. It's the buy/sell decisions made by these funds, along with hedge funds, private equity funds, and pension funds that truly determine the price of a stock.

When the individual investor buys a few hundred shares of a stock they do so at whatever price the market is offering. But when a big hedge fund acquires 0.01% of a company, which might be hundreds of thousands of shares, this act of buying pushes the price up. The same thing happens when they unload a hefty portion of their investment—*they can't get rid of too many shares without driving the price down*. So it makes sense to look at the percent held by institutional investors, and with this metric we want as small a percent as possible. If hardly any of the shares are held by institutional investors, it means that they haven't driven the price up yet. At the same time, a small holding by institutional investors means that there's not much they can unload onto the market—*in order for there to be a big sell-off they would have to buy it first*.

Be leery of any stock that is greater than 80% owned by institutional investors. Granted, this attribute has no impact on the company's profits or their ability to continue paying a dividend, but it could be an indication that the company is overpriced. If high institutional ownership is coupled with a high P/E ratio, it's best to stay away. If you like the company but don't care to purchase them at too high a price, simply add them to your watch list and see if you can get in at a lower price after the institutional investors reduce their holdings.

Short % of Float – This is another attribute that gives us a glimpse into what other investors might already know. But before we delve into how this attribute can be used to our advantage, I want to recommend that you never take a short position in a stock. If you're unfamiliar with the term, *then good!* It's a tool that should only be used by skilled hedgers, but is commonly used by gamblers. It has no place inside the typical retirement portfolio. But for the sake of thoroughness, I'll provide an explanation.

Short selling is the practice of selling a stock before you buy it, and then later closing out the position by making a purchase of the stock. Basically, it's buying and selling in reverse, and in order to make a profit off of a short sale the stock price needs to go down. So you're not investing in a company that you like, but instead are betting against a company's stock. The short seller by his own will is putting himself in a position where the upside potential is limited to the price of the stock, yet the downside potential is completely unlimited. The stock could triple in value and somewhere along the line his broker is going to close the position and send him a bill.

But just because we don't want to sell short doesn't mean that information on short positions isn't useful. By reviewing the percent of a company's shares that are sold short we can attempt to gauge what other investors think of the stock price. If less than 2% of the shares are sold short it tells us that other investors aren't concerned with the outlook (or they're at least not so concerned that they're going to bet against the stock). This, combined with other information, could persuade us to buy. But if we see that 10% of the stock is being sold short it means that others are betting against it and we should proceed with extreme caution. It doesn't matter if we don't know why so much of the stock is being sold short; *it's an indication that the other investors know something that we don't.* As a general rule, if more than 3% of the outstanding shares are being sold short, be cautious. If the short % of float gets up around 5%, it's best to just stay away.

If you like the company and believe that a recent influx of short sellers is simply an indication that the stock is overpriced, add the company to your watch list and see if you can get in at a lower price after the short sellers close their positions. I, however, don't recommend joining the short sellers in an effort to profit from a short-term drop in price. Just because a stock is expensive and overdue for a correction doesn't mean that the correction is coming anytime soon. It's extremely difficult to predict when a justified change in price will actually occur. That's why the strategies discussed in *Dividend Investing* focus on long-term goals rather than short-term movements.

Profile and News – *Yahoo! Finance* publishes a profile and links to news articles for just about every stock out there. The attributes we've discussed are all quantifiable, but your research needs to encompass so much more than this. The profile will tell you exactly what you would expect it to. It lists the sector and industry that the stock belongs to, what their specific services and products are, the brands they own, where the headquarters is located, and of course a link to their website.

News articles are especially important. Not everything that affects the price of a stock is going to make the front page, so it's important to get out there and find out what's being reported about the company. Yes, it's imperative to do quantifiable analysis like comparing P/E ratios and profit margins, but it's also important to understand that not all information that affects the stock price is found in the financial statements. *Has the company announced a new product release? Is there pending litigation? Did they just get a patent approval? Or did a patent just expire? Will the next round of tariffs hurt them? Or will the tariff benefit them at the detriment of a different sector?* These are things you need to know before making an investment. And you need to continue reading after you've bought the stock. This is the reason that I recommend limiting your individual holdings. Somewhere in the neighborhood of five investments should be sufficient. Otherwise, it becomes a tremendous amount of work.

Additional Attributes to Consider When Selecting Dividend Stocks

The attributes we've discussed are important when considering an investment in any stock. But the dividend investor has more work to do. The following attributes pertain directly to stocks that pay dividends.

Dividend Yield – This is the dividend payment measured as a percent of the stock price. If a stock sells for $5.00 and the company distributes quarterly dividends of $0.05, then the dividend yield is 4% (0.05 x 4 / 5 = 0.04). The yield is expressed in terms of total annual payments, but most companies distribute their dividends quarterly.

As dividend investors we are attracted to a high yield, but we know that it's dangerous to chase after the wrong investment just because we like the distribution. As discussed with the Dividend Aristocrats, a long-term investor should be attracted to a stock with a sustainable dividend that increases over time. The yield on the current stock price is only a consideration to new investors. The yield on the price initially paid for the stock becomes increasingly more important as new investors evolve into long-term holders.

Payout Ratio – This is our primary gauge for a sustainable dividend. The payout ratio is the percent of net income that is being distributed. If net income is $2.00 per share and the company pays a $0.27 quarterly dividend, then the payout ratio is 54% (0.27 x 4 / 2). The lower the payout ratio, the better. If it only takes a small percent of the company's earnings to distribute the dividend, then the dividend is considered sustainable. I recommend only buying companies with a payout ratio of 75% or less. Once they exceed this amount it becomes difficult for the company to keep increasing their dividend during economic downturns or any situation that causes net income to suffer. If you can find a payout ratio much smaller than 75%, *even better!* A payout ratio of 30%, for example, is considered attractive.

Cash Flow – While a healthy payout ratio is crucial, it's also important for the company to collect on their earnings. Just about every publicly traded company does its accounting on an accrual basis, meaning that earnings are recognized on sales, not on the receipt of cash. Some of those sales might be collected on immediately, while others sit in accounts receivable and are aged over an extended period of time. So while the payout ratio is the most important measure, I recommend taking a look at the company's cash flow to ensure that enough money is coming in to sustain the dividend payment. If cash flow isn't keeping pace with sales, it could spell trouble. Generally, if the cash flow from operating activities is 125% or more of the dividend payment, then the dividend is thought to be safe.

We won't be dissecting the cash flow statement as we did with the income statement and balance sheet. While the entire statement should be reviewed before making an investment, for our purposes we're going to hone in on a key figure. The cash flow from operating activities tells us how much money the company brought in from their core activities (as opposed to money that comes and goes through their investing and financing activities). The reason we evaluate the dividend based on operating activities is simple, we don't want to invest in a company that has to borrow to pay their dividend. We want a company that brings in real money through its core operations, and then distributes a portion of that money to shareholders. If cash flow from operating activities is at least 125% of the dividend payment, it's an indication of sustainability, particularly if the company is increasing its retained earnings year after year.

Moving Forward

The attributes we've discussed aren't just important when selecting a stock, but should also be used to monitor your stocks after they've been purchased. Companies change with time and the shareholders should stay informed. You need to know if earnings are increasing or decreasing, if more of the stock is being sold short, or if the payout ratio has changed. If the company starts taking on more long-term debt you need to determine if it's because they have promising new projects or if they're having cash flow problems. A successful stock picker keeps up on everything. And this is precisely why I recommend making index funds the bulk of the portfolio. If you're driven to do this work, do it with a small percentage of your portfolio in an effort to gain an edge over the market.

Chapter 7

Don't Chase After High Yields

One of the biggest mistakes that an investor can make is getting suckered into a bad investment because of an attractive dividend yield. I've alluded to this mistake, but have yet to define what constitutes a high yield. That's because there's no precise definition. Growth stocks on average will have lower dividend yields than blue chips, for example, and stocks that belong to a certain sector may exhibit payout characteristics that are vastly different from those of stocks in a different sector. REITs, when compared to stocks, will on average provide higher yields. That's because the IRS requires them to distribute at least 90% of their earnings. So when evaluating an investment to determine if the dividend is unrealistically high, it needs to be evaluated in terms of the sector or asset class that it belongs to.

If we want to set a general benchmark for dividend stocks, we can refer to the Dividend Aristocrats. This means that we compare a company's dividend yield to that of a group of stocks that provide sustainable dividends. At the time of writing the average yield of the Dividend Aristocrats is 2.4%. The average payout ratio is 46%. This doesn't specifically mean that a stock yielding more than 2.4% with a payout ratio above 46% is a bad investment. It simply means that the higher the yield and payout ratio of a stock in comparison to that of the index average, the greater the chance that the investment is risky. And there's nothing wrong with adding risk to the portfolio, so long as the risk is controlled. When we get to *Chapter 11: Asset Allocation*, we'll focus on ways to control for risk. Right now, we want to understand that while high yields are tempting, we don't want to build a portfolio comprised of nothing but high yielding investments. We shouldn't chase stocks simply because of their dividends; rather, we want to select carefully from the available dividend payers should we choose to include individual stocks in our portfolio.

Perhaps an example will help. At the time of writing AT&T Inc. (T) has the highest dividend yield of all the Dividend Aristocrats. It currently offers 6.3%, and there are plenty of investors out there who find this tempting. Exxon Mobile (XOM) has the highest payout ratio of all 53 stocks in the index. It sits at 63.75%, which is still below our maximum threshold of 75%. Both companies have lagged the S&P 500 in the two years following the 2016 presidential election, with AT&T Inc. (T) falling 14% and Exxon Mobile (XOM) falling 6%. At the same time, the S&P 500 rose 30%. In contrast, Roper Technologies Inc. (ROP) had the lowest yield and payout ratio of any company in the index. The stock only yields 0.60%, and the payout ratio sits at 15.4%. It appreciated in value by 62% over the same two-year period, leaving AT&T Inc. (T) and Exxon Mobile (XOM) in the dust.

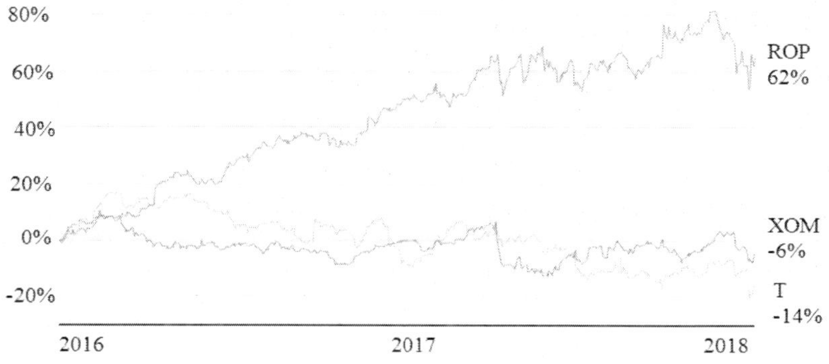

Dividends are important from a compounding perspective, but a high yield should not be viewed as the be-all-end-all of an investment. Certainly, it's nice to earn more than the 0.60% offered by Roper Technologies Inc. (ROP), but it's next to impossible to compensate for an extra 32% over the market during a two-year period. We're never going to know in advance which stock, if any, is going to beat the index by 32%. If we did then we wouldn't bother diversifying, we'd simply put all of our eggs in one basket. But if we recognize the dangers of chasing a stock purely for its yield, then we can diversify into other stocks that don't present that kind of danger. Diversification allows us to include stocks like Roper Technologies Inc. (ROP) that offer a lower yield, while the greater portfolio can maintain a yield closer to the average of the index funds it holds. My advice is to include both low and high yield stocks in the portfolio, so long as other indications for success are present. Not every high yielder turns out like AT&T Inc. (T) or Exxon Mobile (XOM). In fact, buying a high yielder after it's been beaten down can be rewarding. If they are a strong yet under-priced company, buying up their stock after a correction makes sense. I'm not making a specific recommendation for either AT&T Inc. (T) or Exxon Mobile (XOM), but rather reiterating that past performance is not an indication of future performance. That, and both companies happen to be trading below their 200-day moving average at the time of writing.

On average, growth stocks will yield less than the blue chips. And it's okay to buy into a stock that only pays 1% or so. Even 0.60% is acceptable. And the stock doesn't have to go through the ringer just because it offers a low yield. The best dividend plays don't necessarily offer tempting yields, but it's crucial for them to offer sustainable payments. When held for the long-term, what started out as a low dividend can easily yield double digits against your initial investment. And that's the kind of yield that you'll have to wait for rather than chase after. Not every stock will do this, but that's the point of diversification. For every stock that cuts its dividend and flounders off into oblivion you should be holding other stocks and funds that more than offset the impact. That's the power of indexing. One investment can provide exposure to 500 or more stocks. If a handful of stocks that comprise a large index stop paying dividends, the fundholder will never even feel the impact. But when you make a small selection of individual stocks, it's different. You'll feel it when a company stops paying its dividend. So it's important that you favor a safe dividend over a large dividend.

When it comes to individual stocks, the investor should feel comfortable accepting a higher yield from a mature company with less room for growth. But getting to the point where you're yielding double digits off the initial investment is a waiting game. It's a huge red flag when a stock yields anywhere close to 10% against its current selling price. This type of investment should be avoided at all cost.

As I stated before, if you enjoy investing in individual stocks, my recommendation is that they comprise a small percent of the portfolio. And you should be prepared for them to take up a large percent of your time. If you can use them to get that extra edge over market, no matter how small, you'll see the benefits compound in your favor. But even with your index funds—*which by definition track the market*—you can still gain an advantage. When we get to *Chapter 12: Rebalancing* we'll discuss exactly how that works.

If the previous sections on individual stock selection were painful to read, then it's okay to stick 100% with index funds.

When invested in the right markets for an extended period of time your rewards won't just be gainful, they'll be safe and reliable. This is our ultimate goal, and it's incredibly easy to achieve.

Chapter 8

A Bear Market is the Dividend Investor's Best Friend

A bear market is defined as a market condition in which security prices fall 20% or more from their most recent top. And it generally doesn't stop there. The average decline during a bear market is 33%. Bear market conditions are significantly "worse" than the typical correction, which is defined as a 10% pullback. A correction can be expected to occur about once every year or two. I placed quotation marks around the word "worse" because the market going down isn't necessarily bad. In fact, you should expect to encounter a bear market several times throughout your investing career. It's just that we don't know when. And yes, a bear market definitely means that most portfolios are immediately valued at less than their previous worth. It's a natural consequence of there being more sellers than buyers. The investor whose strategy consists of hoping the market always goes up is likely to find such conditions unpleasant. But the smart money understands that a bear market makes for incredible buying opportunities. The difficult part is determining when to get out before the bear comes, while also being able to get back in somewhere close to the bottom. For those who try to follow the smart money, it comes down to understanding the duration of the average market cycle, and then attempting to time it based on market indicators.

A bear market can last anywhere from several weeks to many years, but on average will persist for fourteen months before a new bull emerges. Most 10% corrections, on the other hand, are resolved quickly, typically within a month or two. But it's possible for a correction to last longer without officially slipping into bear territory. Between 1959 and

1960 the market declined 14% and remained in correction mode for 422 days before a new bull emerged. An even closer brush with bear territory occurred between 1976 and 1978, when the market declined 19% and took 531 days to recover.

What makes a correction so perplexing is that investors never really know if it's just a correction or if instead it's the start of a bear market. When the correction isn't resolved quickly, investors are prone to become speculators. *Should I buy the dip? Or do I pull my money out before it goes lower?* The strategy I'm going to recommend evades these questions. It's based on profiting from long-term market cycles without having to make judgment calls based on market conditions. The first step is to understand how a bear market works and why you should not be afraid of the bear. The conditions have not gotten "worse" during a bear market; rather, the conditions are what we should expect them to be at various stages throughout our investment horizon. And if we understand this, then we can see that a bear is truly the dividend investor's best friend, especially when it's encountered early on.

We've already discussed reversion to the mean and why it's beneficial to buy a stock below its 200-day moving average. During a bear market it's not just individual stocks, but most indexes that are trading below their 200-day moving average, and they will do so for a prolonged period of time. Our strategy isn't about trying to time our way out of a top so we can get back in at the bottom. These tactics are subject to human error and emotional thinking. But when a market is in full bear mode, it's easy to determine that securities are cheap, and if we'll be holding them for at least five years, but preferably longer, then there should be a sense of safety when buying stocks in these conditions.

As dividend investors we love strong yields. And we know that it always pays to be patient. A strong investment that will increase its yield annually is more reliable than a speculative investment that offers a high yield today. The fact that the dividend yield is inversely related to the stock price means that the yield on a new investment goes up during a bear market. This, of course, assumes that the economic conditions haven't forced companies to cut their dividends. Some will. But when buying an index fund that holds the greater market, such as the S&P 500 or the Dividend Aristocrats, our chances are good that the dividend yield for new investors will increase as prices are beaten down. There are enough strong stocks in the S&P 500 to offset those who cut their dividend. And if a company belongs to the Dividend Aristocrats, then they have a long track record of increasing their dividend through both positive and negative economic conditions.

The wait for a stronger yield on the cost of your initial investment is much shorter when securities are purchased during a bear market. If stocks have been beaten down, you not only get in when the price is attractive, but also when the yield is attractive. This not only translates into larger dividend payments, but larger capital gains.

If you're just starting to build a portfolio, a bear market is the perfect environment. The new money that you throw in is put to great use, and you don't have to watch your older investments get raked over the coals. But if you do have existing investments, it means you also have dividend income. And though it might be painful to watch the value of your portfolio depreciate (albeit temporarily), this is a great environment for reinvesting those dividends. We already know that the benefit of compounding our dividends over the course of our working years is tremendous. In our example from *Chapter 2: Compound Interest*, our investor was better off by $355,122 come retirement because of compounded dividend income. In this example we assumed that the dividends were reinvested in market conditions that conform to our average expected yearly return (in other words, we assumed average appreciation along a straight line). In reality markets will exhibit volatility as they progress towards a long-term return that should be similar to what we expect. When markets are down, you're not just getting in at a lower price, you're also acquiring more shares.

If you have $1,000 in dividend income to reinvest in a security that sells for $25 per share, you will acquire 40 shares. But if a bear market comes along and pulls the price down to $20, that same $1,000 will now buy 50 shares.

1,000 / 25 = 40

1,000 / 20 = 50

The fact that dividends are paid per share is important. Let's say the security pays a $0.30 quarterly dividend. This provides a 4.8% yield when the security sells for $25. Your quarterly payments will be $12.

(0.30 x 4) / 25 = 4.8%

40 x 0.30 = 12

But when the security drops to $20, your new investment will yield 6% and provide a quarterly payment of $15.

(0.30 x 4) / 20 = 6.0%

50 x 0.30 = 15

That's an extra $3 you can earn by reinvesting your dividends in a bear market. But it's not just a one-time payment of $3. Because the market went down, you now get an extra $3 every quarter. And if the market is still down the next time you reinvest $1,000 in dividend income (though next time it really should be $1,015, not $1,000), you'll earn another $3 per quarter. And as each of those $3 add-ons is included in the act of reinvesting your dividends, you begin to earn distributions on them as well.

In this example, had the market gone up instead of down, and the security moved from $25 to $30 per share, your $1,000 in dividend income would have only bought 33 shares. And the quarterly distribution on those 33 shares would be $9.90. I think we all agree that it's better to compound $15 per quarter for the rest of our lives than to compound $9.90 per quarter. This doesn't mean we won't take the $9.90 when it's being offered. Waiting for a better entry point is dangerous, as markets have the potential to keep going higher. Our strategy is to reinvest our dividends at set intervals regardless of market conditions. But when a bear market comes, there's no reason to be concerned. You should rest assured that your reinvested dividends are being put to good use.

It might feel like just an extra $3. But the market went down instead of up, so you might think of it as an extra $5.10 each quarter (15.00 – 9.90 = 5.10). If you still have 30 years until retirement, it equates to $612 in dividend income (5.10 x 4 x 30 = 612). Yes, this might seem like small potatoes. But that's an extra $612 that you gradually start to compound additional returns off of. It's a small step. But that's what wealth creation is. It's a series of small steps that you repeat over and over again until you're wealthy. If the bear market lasts 18 months (or six quarters), then it's not an extra $612, it's an extra $3,672 (612 x 6 = 3,672).

Speaking of small steps, let's not forget the savings on fees that you'll incur by selecting the right index funds. Or the savings on commissions that you get if you use an online discount broker instead of a full service financial advisor. And every year the dividends paid on your holdings should increase, albeit gradually. These are all small steps that you take concurrently for many, many years. The fact that you'll be investing in strong asset classes is the driving force behind your returns, but every small step that gets repeated over and over again serves as an additional catalyst. When we get to asset allocation and rebalancing in Chapters 11 and 12 we'll discuss some big steps that propel our investments forward. But for now, I want you to see the extra ammunition that a bear market provides.

All of the benefits that accompany a bear market are very recognizable. Securities are sold at a discount. The dividend yields on new purchases are stronger. And the larger distributions from your new securities will compound for the rest of your life (or however long you hold the securities). And while the benefits derived from a bear market are remarkable, we shouldn't forget that there's a cold side that goes along with market declines. In fact, most investors make the mistake of focusing only on the negatives.

The further into your investment horizon you progress, the more damaging a bear market will be if you haven't sought refuge through an increased allocation to bonds. At the same time, in order to continue benefiting from market upturns you must maintain exposure to equities. This is where risk and reward comes into play. A greater allocation to equities will benefit you during market upturns, but you need to be prepared. When the bear comes growling it will take a great big bite out of those equities. When this happens the smartest thing you can do is to just see the bear through. No matter what you do, don't get scared and sell. A bear market is the worst possible environment to unload equities.

The great thing about a bear market early on is that you're just starting to accumulate wealth, so the bear gives you an opportunity to increase your holdings at low prices before your portfolio has gotten big enough for the bear to do considerable damage. Once you've accumulated larger holdings it's a completely different ballgame, and seeing the bear through to the end will be more challenging. This doesn't mean that benefits can't be culled from a bear market later in the game. It just means that those larger dividend yields that you collect on new investments made during a bear market have less time to compound.

As we dive deeper into our investment strategy we'll revisit bear markets in terms of dollar cost averaging, asset allocation, and rebalancing the portfolio. And we'll see the important role that bear markets play as our different holdings move through their cycles.

Chapter 9

Dollar Cost Averaging

In the above example we saw the benefit of reinvesting our dividends during a bear market. The same concept applies to your monthly contribution, except it's likely that this will happen on a grander scale. It takes time to build your way to $1,000 in quarterly dividend income. But your monthly contribution might be different. Maybe it's $200, or $500, or $1,000. Whatever the number, it's important to invest your contribution at least every quarter, if not every month. As I've stated, we're going to invest it automatically regardless of what we think the market is going to do next. That's the premise behind dollar cost averaging. We're going to repeatedly put the same amount of money on the market at the same predetermined intervals. And just like we saw with our reinvested dividends, by doing so we buy more shares when the market is down than we do when the market is up. And this gives us an average purchase price that is lower than the average price that our securities have sold for.

Let's take a closer look. Say, for example, we invest $500 per month in Fund A, and the first month we invest it sells for $20. This will afford us 25 shares. If during the next month the fund takes a big dip and sells for only $15, then our second investment of $500 will afford us 33 shares. The advantage of buying more shares when the market is down is that the average price paid per share is less then the average of $20 and $15.

The average of $15 and $20 is $17.50.

(20 + 15) / 2 = 17.50

However, the average we paid for Fund A is only

$17.25.

500 / 20 = 25

500 / 15 = 33

25 + 33 = 58

1,000 / 58 = 17.25

It might help to think of $17.50 as being similar to the 200-day moving average. This is the average price that the security has sold for during the breadth of our investing. Yet the price we paid for the security averages to only $17.25, all because we bought a larger number of shares during the dip. We can expect the price to revert to its mean (rise back towards $17.50). This will put us in the green. But if it doesn't do so by the time we're ready to make next month's investment, then we'll be buying even more shares at the lower price.

Now, let's suppose that Fund A pays a quarterly dividend of $0.15. Our first investment of $500 bought 25 shares, so we'll start to receive $3.75 per quarter off of our investment (25 x 0.15 = 3.75). Our second investment of $500, however, bought us 33 shares, so we'll receive $4.95 per quarter off of this investment (33 x 0.15 = 4.95). This brings our total quarterly dividend income to $8.70 after only two months of investing.

Of course, we'll want to continue making contributions of $500 each month. This not only progressively increases our dividend income, but allows us to average into an advantageous price. The price of the fund will ebb and flow, but we'll automatically buy more shares when the fund dips than we will when it rises. And this is exactly what we want. We won't attempt to time the market. We can't control what direction the price will move next, and the strategies discussed in *Dividend Investing* are based on controlling for variables that can actually be controlled. We can control whether or not we continue to contribute $500 each month. We can control whether or not we automatically purchase Fund A each month regardless of what has happened to the price and where we think the price will go next. And we should continue to do this because we know that this will average us into a beneficial price and have a positive impact on our dividend yield. But there's one more thing we can control for, and that's whether or not we reinvest the dividends. It might take a few quarters, but our dividend income will eventually exceed the cost of an additional share, so we'll eventually start investing $500 per month along with whatever dividend income has accumulated in the portfolio. And this has a two-pronged effect. Not only do we enjoy the benefits of compounding, but we align those benefits with a dollar cost averaging approach so that our reinvested dividends will also buy more shares when the market dips than they will when the market rises. The result is that our average cost per share, from both contributed capital and reinvested dividends, is less than the average price that the fund has sold for, simply because we're acquiring more shares when the price is low. This puts the odds in our favor, not just with Fund A, but with every fund we purchase.

What we really want is to watch our investments gradually (*if not rapidly*) increase in value. And while a gradual increase is realistic, it's not realistic for it to appreciate in a straight line. There will be dips along the way. An approach that combines dollar cost averaging with reinvested dividends makes us better off for experiencing those dips. It's not pleasant to watch our portfolio decline in value, but we're not just holding investments—*we're progressively adding to them.* From a buying perspective, the dips are good. And a drop that is deeper than a dip is even better. Those extended downward movements give us an opportunity to both buy and reinvest at a discount (sometimes for extended durations), and we already know that by doing so we drive up our dividend yields. The benefits will compound and reward us indefinitely. It's all about staying in the market and controlling for the variables over which we have control. We have control over making our monthly contributions and systematically investing in the market regardless of where it's gone or where we think it might go next. But we don't have any control over market movements, and we're better off if we don't try to predict them. A dollar cost averaging strategy removes all guesswork from the equation. We buy when markets go up. We buy when markets go down. And we do so without hesitation.

It's during extended bear markets that dividend stocks truly beat growth stocks. People seek refuge in dividend payers when markets are down. But that doesn't mean we don't want both kinds of stocks in the portfolio at all times, *because we do*. Again, we're not attempting to time the market and we don't want to switch entirely from growth stocks to dividend stocks (or vice-versa) based on predictions of when a bear market (or bull market) is about to begin.

As we dollar cost average we will contribute not just to a single fund, but to a variety of funds. While Fund A might be a lucrative fund to invest in, we still want diversification. So if we have $500 to invest each month, we might put $200 in a growth fund, $100 in a dividend fund, $100 in a bond fund, and the remaining $100 in a real estate fund. We're now invested in different markets. And these markets aren't all going to move in the same direction at the same time. Our stock funds might edge up as our real estate fund takes a dip. But we'll continue to dollar cost average in the manner we determined prior to these market movements. It might seem more lucrative to place a larger allocation into real estate, perhaps $200 instead of $100. We know that dividend yields get larger when a market slumps, so in this example it's tempting to buy more real estate. We'll increase our dividend income by doing so. And we're also buying the real estate at a lower price, so over the long-haul we should expect larger capital gains. But we're not going to do this, because when we try to predict market direction our results become prone to human error, and we want to avoid this at all cost. In later chapters we'll add elements to the strategy that allow us to benefit from these movements without having to time the market. Everything we do will be implemented systematically, and will remove all guess-work from the equation.

When we dollar cost average, we never want to adjust the contribution to each fund based on market direction. We won't allocate more to a fund because the market has gone down and looks like a bargain. We also won't allocate more to a fund because it looks like the market will keep going up. Instead, we'll determine in advance how much to allocate to each fund, and we'll specify the intervals in which the investments will be made. Then we'll stick to it. In this example we are going to allocate $200 to a growth fund, $100 to a dividend fund, $100 to a bond fund, and the remaining $100 to a real estate fund. Every month when we invest our $500, this is how we do it. And as we accrue dividend income, we're going to reinvest it proportionately along with the contribution. If we receive $50 in dividends, we'll reinvest $20 into our growth fund and $10 into each of our other funds. The approach is systematic and does not require us to predict market direction. Over time this will force us to average into a lucrative price for each of the funds that we're invested in.

In coming chapters we'll explore a systematic approach that allows us to take advantage of the dips without having to predict market direction. In *Chapter 11: Asset Allocation* we'll learn how to automatically buy low and sell high as we keep the portfolio balanced. And we'll do this in a manner that builds on our dollar cost averaging strategy. But first let's take a look at the different markets that we'll be investing in. There's an advantage to diversifying across markets that react differently to changes in the economic environment. And there's an even greater advantage to investing in markets that have a history of always beating inflation over extended periods of time.

Chapter 10

Diversification

We've covered the benefits of investing in dividend paying securities from the perspective of functionality. *They compound over time!* If we make the right investments, then our dividend income will increase each year irrespective of any new investments that we make. And if we buy when markets are down, we start off with a stronger yield. There are huge benefits to investing in markets that pay dividends, but the functionality of a dividend becomes worthless if the entire portfolio declines in value and never comes back. It's okay, even expected, for certain funds to decline in value and then have to claw their way back into the green. We expect the value of our portfolio to fluctuate. But if the entire portfolio takes a dive and doesn't come back for a very long time, then we've lost years of growth and it's impossible to offset the damage with dividend payments.

That's why we're not just going to invest in the stock market, but in a variety of markets. And within each of these markets we'll find opportunities to gain exposure to different sectors and regions that don't always behave the same way. Our goal is to accumulate wealth. The bigger the pie, the larger our dividend payments will be at retirement. More specifically, we want to stay invested for the long-haul while spreading our risk across many different asset classes, all the while keeping fees low as we control for risk and, to the extent possible, taxes. It all starts with diversification. And it's vital that we not just diversify within a market, but that we diversify across markets.

The more asset classes we invest in (to a point) the greater the reduction of risk. For example, if we invest in 1,000 different stocks and nothing else, we have diversified away the risk of a single company going out of business. If one stock out of 1,000 becomes worthless, the sum of the returns on the other 999 companies more than offsets the loss. So what we are left with is market risk, and this is the risk that the entire stock market will crash (which it does, periodically). It's impossible to eliminate market risk by adding more stocks to our portfolio. By using an index fund approach we already have exposure to the entire stock market. And by keeping the combined weight of our individual stock selections to 5%, we control for the impact that a single company can have on the greater portfolio. We might spend a great deal of time tracking our individual holdings in an effort to get an edge over the market, but when it comes to the greater portfolio we're really not concerned with the happenings of a single company. It's tempting to daydream about having allocated 20% of the portfolio to Amazon.com Inc. (AMZN) before the stock shot through the roof. But this type of growth can neither be predicted nor sustained. Even if net income continues to increase, there's always a possibility that the stock will be viewed as overpriced and will fall hard. The approach discussed in *Dividend Investing* is focused on eliminating this type of high risk-high reward scenario, in favor of collecting dividends as our wealth steadily increases.

We can reduce and eliminate risk that is specific to an individual company by holding an index fund that is representative of the greater market. But to control for risk that pertains to the market, we have to simultaneously invest in other markets. As dividend investors we want to invest in securities that offer a distribution. The bond market offers interest and the real estate market pays rent. Even though these distributions are not technically dividends, from a compounding perspective they function just the same. From a tax perspective, there are major differences, and depending on the type of account you hold your investments in, it's possible to eliminate the differences. We cannot, however, forgo proper diversification for the sake of taxes. Interest is taxed heavier than most dividends. And real estate investments have very complex tax implications. When we throw foreign investments into the mix, planning for taxes becomes even more complex. But we're not going to structure our asset allocation around tax consequences. We will first control for risk through proper diversification, and then take measures to reduce taxes where possible. If we do it the other way around we risk poor performance for the sake of reducing our tax bill. It's better to perform well and pay the taxes than to let an aversion to taxes stifle your performance. So we will include stocks, bonds, and real estate in our portfolio in proportions that provide strong returns while controlling for risk. And if we are able to control for taxes without infringing on our market-driven approach, we will add additional controls.

It should also be noted that too many asset classes will have an adverse affect on the portfolio. It's generally accepted that holding more than twelve asset classes will reduce the benefits of diversification. Our rebalancing strategy is going to force us to buy low and sell high. So long as our holdings are finite we can rebalance in a way that's meaningful, and this permits us to reap rewards. But extreme diversification often leads to diminished returns, because your winners won't stand out, and your losers don't get proper nourishment, so to speak. We're going to learn how to take gains and redistribute them back into investments that are underpriced. But if we hold too many markets, the gains will be redistributed too thinly and the benefit will be minimal. This, coupled with the additional transaction costs of rebalancing too many asset classes can hurt the portfolio. It's better to error on the side of holding too few asset classes, and so long as we maintain broad exposure to stocks, bonds, and real estate, there's little to worry about. Of course, there's room to gain additional exposure by branching off into subclasses. This allows us to weight our exposure in favor of different sectors or regions that are expected to provide the greatest benefit. I only caution that the total number of funds invested in be limited to 12 at most. And for the new investor starting off with a small portfolio, it's perfectly fine to invest in an even smaller group of funds.

Asset Classes

Stocks, bonds, and real estate. I hope I've made it sound simple so far, because it really is. We're going to buy three different asset classes to hold for the long-haul as we reinvest our dividends. And if you're ready to call it a day and go take a nap, we're actually not too far from reaching the point where you can do that. That's the benefit of investing in entire markets. I'll teach you some tricks to gain an edge on those markets, and it won't be nearly as difficult as picking your own stocks.

But before we dive deeper into strategy, let's have a close look at the markets we'll be investing in.

Stocks

The stock market, of course, is the most recognized investment market. When someone says they're invested in "the market", stocks are what you think of first. And while many markets exist, an exorbitant proportion of retirement savings is invested in the stock market. From a risk-reward standpoint, this is one of the riskier asset classes available, yet the stock market has a history of always bouncing back from its lows. It has a history of always beating inflation when invested in for long periods of time, with the average return for the S&P 500 being 10% annually when invested in for ten years. But if 10% is the average, it means that approximately half the time, returns are below 10%.

While index funds should serve as the nucleus of the portfolio, a domestic large cap fund should serve as the nucleus of the stock holdings. We also want growth, especially early on, so there should be room in the portfolio for a growth fund. But there is both stability and yield when it comes to large cap stocks. And for this reason I recommend exposure to either the S&P 500 or the Dividend Aristocrats. While the S&P 500 holds approximately 10 times more stocks, the Dividend Aristocrats have exhibited comparative performance since the inception of the index in 1989, but with a stronger dividend yield. It's not a dangerous yield, simply a higher yield. And this is a case where I recommend chasing the higher yield for better long-term results.

A growth fund should then be added, and exposure to small-cap stocks might be desired. Some investors choose to hold a small-cap growth fund, as both growth funds and small-cap funds have a history of providing better long-term returns than do most blue chip funds. But when the market goes down, growth stocks and small-cap stocks generally decline by more than the blue chips. This is why we want exposure to different types of stocks. And when we get to *Chapter 12: Rebalancing*, we'll see that there's an advantage to holding them in separate funds, rather than buying a single fund that holds the entire U.S. stock market. We want to maintain no more than 12 holdings, and a younger portfolio might only start off with three funds. But options for further weighting the portfolio in favor of dividend players are extensive. Many investors will select an index fund that tracks a specific sector, and by holding that fund in addition to the S&P 500 or the Dividend Aristocrats, the overall portfolio is then heavier weighted in favor of that sector.

Sectors

The S&P 500 consists of 11 different sectors, and there are a variety of ETFs available that not only provide exposure to each of those sectors, but also ones that provide exposure to subsectors. The benefits (and risks) of investing in different sectors or subsectors will, of course, vary by sector and investment objective. As dividend investors we want to hone in on sectors that pay steady and reliable dividends. And where we can get a yield that beats that of the S&P 500, then we should take a closer look to determine if exposure to the sector is appropriate given the other holdings in the portfolio.

Historically, the dividend rich sectors have included utilities, financials, energy, and telecom. And while dividend income may be the ultimate goal, each sector has other characteristics that drive their performance.

Utility Stocks

Utility stocks are categorized as defensive stocks. Even during economic downturns people still use utilities. And these are really good for diversification because defensive stocks don't adhere to a business cycle. People will rush into them when a downturn is expected, and flee from them when they think the bull is ready to emerge. But this is merely investor behavior. The customers still require year-round service. At the time of writing, funds that track utilities are yielding a tad higher than 3%. This will provide an edge over the market at certain points in the cycle, and can also be used to increase yield in retirement when capital gains aren't as important. Like other defensive stocks, they are for the risk-adverse investor who is looking for a steady stream of dividend income.

Financial Stocks

Financials is the only sector that has a history of beating utilities in terms of yield. Since the financial crises, large-cap bank stocks have been especially attractive to dividend investors, and these companies are likely to weather any storm because they are holding on to large cash reserves. Given the amount of business generated off of mortgages and other loans, this sector outperforms when interest rates are low. Unlike utilities, financial stocks adhere to a very observable, though not predictable, business cycle. They perform best when the economy is in an upswing, as this is when businesses demand loans for new projects. In fact, economists often use financial stocks as a barometer for the health of the overall economy. At the time of writing, the financials sector is actually yielding less than utilities, coming in with an average yield that's just a tad under 3%. Historically, financials have yielded closer to 4%, with REIT, mortgage, and asset management services pulling up the average.

Energy Stocks

Like the financials sector, energy stocks are characterized by conforming to a very observable, though not predictable, business cycle. Their performance is mainly tied to the worldwide demand for oil and gas, and there are index funds available to track performance at each stage of the supply chain. Where one investor might go for companies involved in oil and gas exploration and production, another might chase after companies in the coal industry. And environmentally conscious consumers are more likely to not only use, but to invest in, alternative forms of energy. Overall, the sector is currently yielding approximately 2.5%, but within the different industries that comprise the sector, substantially higher yielding ETFs are available.

Telecom Stocks

Telecom companies are the ones that make communication possible. And due to our reliance on communication and data transmission, there is a perception of safety in this sector. It provides a unique combination of dividend income and growth. At the top are a handful of major players, offering cell phone and Internet service, and paying high dividends in the process. But there are many small companies that produce the equipment needed to provide these services. While it takes a huge capital investment to establish your company as a major Internet provider, there are low barriers to entry when it comes to manufacturing routers and other equipment, or simply performing repairs. There's tremendous potential for growth, and funds that cover the entire sector are able to provide a strong yield along with that growth. ETFs that focus on domestic companies are currently yielding just under 3%, but some ETFs with foreign exposure are yielding greater than 4%.

Portfolio Structure

While dividend yield is important, we also want to be certain that a sector fits properly in the portfolio given our other holdings. The telecom sector, for example, might be a nice compliment to someone also invested in utilities, because utilities are defensive and the telecom sector provides growth. The financials sector, on the other hand, tends to move in unison with the greater market, and therefore doesn't serve as a strong addition to a portfolio that is already heavily invested in the S&P 500. Given that financials typically provide larger dividend yields than the market, moderate exposure may be warranted. The overarching goal is for the portfolio to be well diversified across different markets, with a heavier reliance on the market sectors that benefit us the most. While each fund is intended to provide a yield, we don't want to pair funds together that perform the same in terms of movement. Aside from owning a specific sector, there are other stock fund options that provide yields greater than that of the S&P 500. We've already taken a look at the Dividend Aristocrats, which is a great way to increase yield while maintaining exposure to all 11 sectors of the S&P 500. A preferred stock fund is another way to increase yield. And these funds often yield substantially more than the Dividend Aristocrats.

Preferred Stock

One of the drawbacks of investing in the stock market is that companies are not required to distribute a dividend. If the company wants to keep the funds in-house, they can. As investors, we use diversification as a means of mitigating the impact of a single company cutting or discontinuing their dividend, but nonetheless, your dividend distributions are not guaranteed. That's one of the reasons why it's important to simultaneously invest in other markets. REITs are required to distribute their rental income, and bondholders have rights to their interest payments. Stockholders, on the other hand, can be cut off from receiving a distribution at any time.

Distributions on common shares are issued at the discretion of the company.

Preferred shareholders, on the other hand, have rights. When companies issue preferred stock they give their preferred shareholders distribution rights over those of their common shareholders. This means the company cannot pay a dividend to common shareholders until the preferred shareholders receive their payment. If things go bad for the company and they put their dividend on hold, the preferred shareholders will be paid in arrears—*that is, they will receive back payment for all dividends missed*—before the company can resume their common stock dividends. On top of this, the dividend paid to preferred shareholders is often larger than the dividend paid to common shareholders.

This form of issue is attractive to the investor seeking yield, not growth. In fact, you'll get a stronger distribution with most preferred stock funds than you will with the Dividend Aristocrats. This is because preferred stock funds tend to seek exposure from the higher yielding sectors, such as utilities, financials, energy, and telecom. The distribution from a preferred stock fund is therefore contingent on the distribution from the preferred shares of companies in these sectors. But the movement of preferred stocks is detached from the movement of common stocks. It's the common stock that the public buys when investing in these sectors. And depending on which sector(s) they invest in, their expectation for gains and losses will vary. A defensive utility stock will perform differently than the stock of a bank or mortgage company. The dividend is higher, but the price is somewhat stagnant. It might help to think of preferred shares as an issuance of debt that's packaged as a stock, and the capital gains are resultantly lost in this process. While the price of a preferred share can fluctuate, it generally trades within a few dollars of the issue price. In this regard it truly functions more like debt than equity.

Preferred shares in general are only issued to institutional buyers, meaning you can't just log into your discount brokerage account and buy them up. What you can do is invest in an ETF the holds preferred stock in many companies. And there's safety in numbers. While holding a preferred stock fund does not make your portfolio diversified, it does provide insulation against the risk of holding just one company. This is a relatively safe way to chase after those higher yields, so long as the greater portfolio is diversified across other markets.

From a compounding standpoint, a conservative allocation to preferred stock makes sense, even in the early stages. As the investor nears retirement, there is a benefit to increasing that exposure. Growth will become less important, and the investor who is either at or near retirement will desire the largest cash distributions they can get without sacrificing their capital. A preferred stock ETF won't get the investor all the way there, but the dividend is strong nonetheless.

The iShares US Preferred Stock ETF (PFF) is a low fee fund that holds the constituents that make up the S&P U.S. Preferred Stock Index. It currently yields 6.3%, and the price has been relatively flat for the past 10 years. If we go back to the financial crisis, we see that preferred stock is also subject to irrational selling out of fear. And though it pays a strong and consistent dividend, the fund has not returned to the valuation level it held prior to the financial crisis. It's important to understand that these types of funds can lose value. The same will apply to any fund. What makes a preferred stock fund different is that they don't have a history of always beating inflation when held for the long-haul. It's a low fee dividend play that shows its true strength through compounding. I recommend that young investors keep the allocation conservative, just as we would with individual holdings, with no more than 2.5% to 5% of the portfolio allocated to preferred stock.

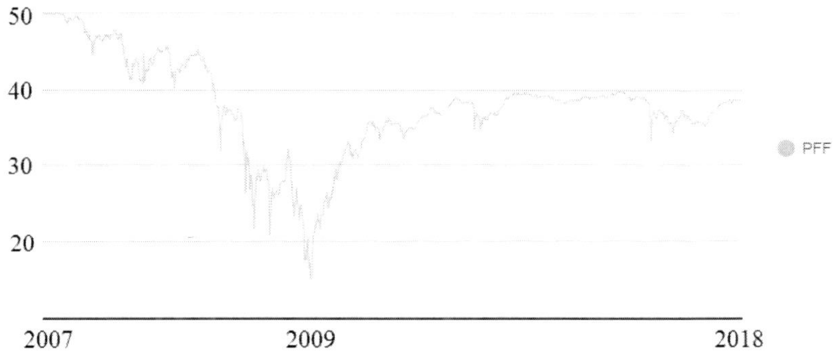

As growth becomes less important and the focus of the portfolio shifts towards income distributions combined with the preservation of capital, it's acceptable to increase the preferred stock allocation. Our expectation is that the fund will provide a strong yield and a stable price. But we need to be aware that a preferred stock fund can be subjected to big hits during recessions. That's why we'll seek other forms of safety within the portfolio. Come retirement, I recommend limiting the preferred stock allocation to no more than 10% of the portfolio.

Strategy

When investing in the stock market we want to select funds that meet two criteria: (1) reliable dividend payments, and (2) long-term gains that exceed the rate of inflation. The stock market, as measured by the performance of the S&P 500, meets these criteria. But when we hone in on individual stocks, sector funds, and preferred stock funds, it's possible to increase yield to the detriment of capital gains. Early on, these high dividend investments should be a very small portion of the portfolio. We're better off with small yields and a lot of growth. But markets move through cycles, and there will be periods when defensive stocks hold their own while growth stocks take a dive. An allocation to bonds aids in providing further protection during market downturns. And while growth stocks provide large leaps and bounds under certain market conditions, it would be foolish to only invest in growth stocks, even if it's early in your investing career.

Initially, the bulk of the stock fund allocation should consist of either the S&P 500 or the Dividend Aristocrats and a growth fund. As time progresses, yield will become more and more important, and while growth is always good, the downside can be risky. Some investors may choose to reduce their allocation to growth stocks in favor of a defensive sector like utilities or a preferred stock fund like PFF. An investor with a high tolerance for risk might prefer to hold growth stocks through the thick and thin.

When we get to *Chapter 11: Asset Allocation*, we'll discuss how much to hold in stocks and real estate and how much to hold in bonds. But within the stock allocation, there's room to customize the holdings to your preferences. Understanding how each sector works, as well as the distinction of a preferred stock fund, will aid in getting the combination of growth, safety, and yield that you prefer.

Bonds

Bonds are an instrument that we use to add safety to the portfolio while maintaining an acceptable stream of income.

And that's it. It all sounds very simple, and if we invest through index funds that simply hold the bond market, than it is very simple. Even determining the weight of the portfolio that should be allocated to bonds is simple. But the mechanics of different bonds, as well as the various tax implications, are anything but simple. Many people never take time to learn about the advantages and disadvantages of different bond issues because the returns are so low. And that makes sense. If you're going to dedicate a lot of time to an endeavor, dedicate it to picking the stocks you think will provide huge returns, not to selecting bonds that might yield just a bit more than the next issue. That's not just my perspective on bonds, it's my perspective on index funds too. It's important to understand what you're investing in and how the markets work. But the beauty of indexing is we don't need to know every little fact about each constituent in the index.

Just like with stocks, we don't want to invest in an actively managed bond fund. We should be content to earn the market average on our bonds because we know that the chances of an actively managed fund consistently beating the market by as much as the fees they charge are very slim. The extra fees paid for active management aren't worth it, and for those funds that do beat the average, it's unlikely that they'll continue to do so indefinitely.

Bond funds are a bit different in that no fund is truly passive. Even a fund that tracks an index only has so many available issues to select from, so ensuring that the fund matches precisely to the underlying index is not always possible. There will always be constituents to a bond index that aren't currently available on a secondary market, and this forces the fund manager to seek the next best alternative. But there's still a huge difference between a bond fund that strives to replicate an index and a bond fund that implements an active management approach.

There are a variety of ETFs available that track different bond indexes, and this allows the investor to hone in on specific grades, maturities, and even regions. We're again looking to keep commissions low by purchasing low fee ETFs through a discount broker.

We'll dig deeper into the different types of bonds, but off the cuff I'm going to recommend overweighting the bond allocation in favor of Treasuries. Bonds issued by the U.S. Government are safer than bonds issued by corporations and foreign governments, mainly because the U.S. Government has the taxing authority to make good on their debt, which keeps the default risk low. And safety is what we're ultimately after. Bonds offset the volatility of stocks. They keep the portfolio as steady as possible. And this can be accomplished entirely with Treasury bonds. Adding a small allotment of investment grade corporate and foreign bonds to the portfolio can help increase yield with only a minor increase in risk. But for the truly risk-adverse investor, holding only Treasury bonds is a perfectly acceptable approach.

Yield

With dividend stocks we know that yield is inversely related to price. When the price of a stock drops, the yield goes up (that is, assuming that the stock price didn't drop as a result of the company cutting the dividend). The same principle applies to bonds, except the issuer isn't at liberty to cut the payment. A bond's return, or yield, is inversely related to its price. As the price of a bond moves up, the quoted yield of the bond moves down. Here, it's not so much the impact of investors buying and selling the bond that moves its price, but changes to the fed funds rate. If interest rates increase, it means that new bond issues will pay more than existing bond issues. Therefore, to sell a bond that you purchased at the old rate, you'll have to sell it at a discount in order to attract buyers. Otherwise, investors will simply buy a newer issue to take advantage of the higher interest payment. The price of a bond (or holding in a bond fund) will always move in the opposite direction of changes to the fed funds rate. When they cut the rate, your bond holdings will increase in value. And when they increase the rate, your bond holdings will decrease in value. Of course, none of this matters if you simply hold a bond to maturity. You'll still get the interest payment you were expecting per the terms of the offering, and any fluctuation in value will be irrelevant once the bond matures; at that point you've received all of your payment and recouped the principal. The value of a bond after maturity is zero.

But we have no intention of buying individual bonds and holding them to maturity. We're going to invest in bond funds, and while we are long-term investors, when we get to *Chapter 12: Rebalancing*, we'll discuss a strategy aimed at increasing the probability of selling our funds at a gain, while picking up other investments at a discount. We like bonds because of their stability, but a little movement in price isn't bad and can work to our advantage.

In fact, the longer the duration of a bond (or in our case, the bonds held in a fund), the greater the movement incurred when interest rates change. This makes sense, because the interest rate on long-term bonds is locked in for a longer period of time. If we buy a 20 year bond at 3.5% and interest rates are immediately cut to 3.0%, we can expect this bond to increase in value by more than a bond with only two years to maturity that also yields 3.5%. *Why?* Because in two years the second bond is going to stop issuing payments at 3.5%, and if interest rates are unchanged between now and then, we'll only be able to reinvest at 3.0%. But our 20 year bond, which still has 18 years to go, will continue to remit payments at 3.5%. By locking in a higher rate for a longer period of time, we gain a greater advantage when interest rates are cut. As before, if we hold the bond until maturity, the increase in value doesn't matter; we simply collect the payments that we were expecting to collect. But should we choose to sell the bond, we can sell it for a gain because it now yields more than the going rate. In fact, the gain will be whatever amount causes the new investor to earn a 3.0% return on their investment. They will pay more for the bond than we did, and though the dollar amount of the interest payments doesn't change, by paying a higher price for the bond their effective return will only be 3.0%. It sounds nice, at least when we're on the selling side of the investment. But changes to the fed funds rate don't always work in our favor.

Had the interest rate been raised to 4.0% rather than cut to 3.5%, the impact would be just the opposite. We'd have locked in a rate that is 0.5% lower than the new going rate. If we want to get out early we'll have to sell the bond at a loss, because an investor would rather buy a new bond at 4.0% than our existing bond at 3.5%. So we'll have to price our bond at a discount in order to attract buyers. Naturally, if our holding is two years until maturity instead of 20, the loss will be smaller, because it won't take as long to reach the point where we can reinvest the funds in a higher yielding bond.

Regardless of direction, when they change the fed funds rate, we'll experience larger price swings with a long-term bond fund than we will with a short-tem bond fund. For this reason, long-term bonds generally offer higher yields than short-term bonds. This is referred to as an interest rate premium.

When investing in the bond market for extended periods of time, we certainly want the extra yield that comes with a long-term holding. But we also want protection when rates move against us. Part of that protection will come from investing in different markets. And part of that protection will come from holding both short-term and long-term bond funds. Each fund will fluctuate in value based on maturity, but when multiple funds are held simultaneously, the portfolio will fluctuate based on the average maturity of the holdings. The purpose of *Dividend Investing* is not to speculate on what direction the interest rate (or the value of bonds or bond funds) will move. Instead, we're simply going to weight our bond fund holdings in favor of our goal. If we're comfortable with risk, we can weight our holdings in favor of long-term bonds. This will provide for a higher yield, and the additional risk will be moderate when compared to increased reliance on stocks and real estate.

Additionally, the bond investor can further increase yield with exposure to corporate bonds and foreign bonds. These issues have additional risk over Treasuries, and therefore must provide higher returns. There's added risk that a corporation or foreign government might default on their bond payments. The higher interest payment on these issues is referred to as a default risk premium. When we hold many bonds we mitigate the risk of a specific corporation or foreign government defaulting on their payment. Therefore, the additional risk is small in comparison to stocks and real estate, but the holdings also won't provide large capital gains (or losses). The best approach to integrating these holdings into the portfolio is through a fund that offers broad market exposure. We can mitigate the risk of a specific corporation or foreign government defaulting on their bonds, but we cannot mitigate economic factors that affect the entire bond market. For this reason, we again need added diversification from both the stock and real estate markets.

Let's take a closer look at the available options. We'll start with Treasuries and then move on to corporate and foreign bonds.

Treasuries

I've instilled the notion that we only want to invest in markets that have a history of always beating inflation over long periods of time. This, of course, stacks the cards in favor of the long-term investor, and it makes the often confusing world of securities a safe place to be.

In all likelihood, bonds will provide the lowest long-term returns of all our asset classes. We buy them for safety knowing that we're sacrificing gains for steady and predictable interest payments. The bond market still provides ample opportunity to beat inflation, but in increments that are much smaller than those achieved through the stock and real estate markets.

Investing in T-bills is the closest you can get to a risk-free investment. T-bills are short-term debt instruments issued by the Treasury Department of the U.S. Government. They mature within 12 months of issue and are often referred to as discount notes. This is because of their payment structure. When you purchase a T-bill you pay less than the par value, or face value. When it matures, you receive the par value. In other words, the difference between the purchase price and the par value is the interest payment, and at maturity you receive both the return of your principal and the interest in one lump sum.

The fact that T-bills are backed by the taxing authority of the U.S Government means that default risk is extremely low. The price still fluctuates in direct proportion to changes in the fed funds rate, because the next safest option is to simply hold cash in an account that pays the going rate of interest. A T-bill therefore insures that your investment keeps pace with inflation, and nothing more.

As we move from T-bills to T-notes and then to T-bonds, the term-to-maturity increases. A T-note is issued with a maturity date between one and ten years, where a T-bond is issued with a maturity date greater than ten years. For our purposes, it's all semantics. Just as interest and rental payments function the same as dividend income, bills, notes, and bonds all function as fixed income debt instruments. As we structure our portfolio we definitely want to pay attention to maturity, but the word "bond" can be used interchangeably to cover all of these instruments. As the term-to-maturity increases, so does the interest rate risk. As a result, long-term bonds will pay higher interest than short-term bonds. There needs to be an incentive for the investor to commit to a longer maturity, as this prevents them from reinvesting in a newer issue when interest rates rise. We know that the T-bill will pay interest that keeps pace with inflation. So anything with a maturity longer than a T-bill should be expected to beat inflation.

When it comes to bonds we're primarily concerned with both the default risk and interest rate risk. And we know that Treasuries are a safe bet for mitigating both of these risks. Your chances of winning the lottery exceed the chances of the U.S. Government defaulting on Treasuries. And interest rate risk is mitigated because the longer the term-to-maturity, the higher the interest rate that must be offered. This helps us beat inflation. But given the longer maturity, there's still a chance that inflation will increase to more than what our bonds are yielding. We control for this through diversification. It's beneficial to invest in different ETFs that hold bonds with varying terms-to-maturity. You can easily select different funds that hold short-term, intermediate-term, and long-term Treasuries. And while the funds will hold bonds of appropriate length, the holdings within the funds are purchased at different times and will have staggering maturity dates. The structure can vary based on the bond index that is being tracked, but a fund that invests in 10 year bonds is likely to have an average maturity date of five years. A 20 year bond fund will likely have an average maturity date of 10 years, and so forth. Again, the longer the duration, the higher the yield. And while we invest in bond funds for the income and safety they provide, it's important to understand that the value of the fund will fluctuate. And this fluctuation in price has an inverse relationship with the fed funds rate.

We know that a short-term fund (T-bills) will match inflation. Given that all of the holdings mature within a year, the price fluctuations will be very small when interest rates change. The intermediate-term fund (T-notes) will offer a yield that beats inflation. But when interest rates rise the fund is immediately at a disadvantage. Because it's an intermediate fund, it will hold a variety of bonds with remaining durations of one to 10 years. Depending on the specific fund, we might assume an average maturity of five years. The fund will progressively replace its maturing bonds with new issues that offer a premium over the current rate of inflation. The same can be observed with a fund that holds long-term Treasuries (T-bonds). It will offer even larger interest payments than the intermediate-term fund, but when interest rates rise, the process of replacing bonds as they mature with new issues will take longer. It should not be assumed that all of the bonds will be held to maturity. Depending on the management style or the nature of the index being tracked, some of the bonds can be sold long before their maturity date. Whether they are sold for a gain or loss depends on the direction that interest rates have moved since the bond was purchased. This will impact the value of the fund, as well as the cash that the fund has available to distribute or reinvest.

Given that both moderate- and long-term funds invest in bonds that offer an interest rate premium, there's insulation when interest rates rise. If your long-term fund yields 0.50% more than inflation and interest rates are raised by 0.25%, the fund is still beating inflation. On top of this, maturing bonds are replaced by new long-term bonds that now pay a higher rate. So each month when you receive your payment from the fund, it will on average be higher than payments from prior months, so long as the fed funds rate is increasing. It all sounds very convenient—*and safe*—yet the potential for a fund to yield less than inflation is very real. Should interest rates keep going up, the payments on either a moderate- or long-term bond fund can start to lag inflation. It takes time for the older issues to cycle through the fund and get replaced. The longer the average duration of a fund, the greater the chances that it could at some point lag inflation. And when it eventually does, the shortfall could persist for years. In most cases, this is just a short-term fallback. Over the long-term, we anticipate that a portfolio invested in a diversified selection of bond funds will provide returns in excess of the average rate of inflation. When your investment horizon is 20, 30, or even 40 years, you're in a very safe position. There might be intermittent periods where your payments sum to less than what is currently provided at the going interest rate, but we account for this by earning higher returns on our long-term holdings throughout the bulk of our investment span. We don't need to beat inflation every quarter or even every year. We need to beat inflation between that dates that we make new investments and dates that we take money off the table. For the long-term investor, this is exceptionally easy.

Earning an interest rate premium helps. But the true advantage to holding long-term bond funds is best observed when interest rates fall. In this case, the interest rate premium doesn't just provide insulation, but insures that we continue to earn more than inflation as rates go down. In this environment, the benefit is instant. If your long-term fund yields 0.50% more than inflation and interest rates are cut (rather than raised) by 0.25%, the fund not only continues to beat inflation, but does so by 0.75% rather than 0.50%. Yes, holdings within the fund are going to mature and be replaced by new lower yielding issues, but the newer bonds still come with an interest rate premium. With interest rates having been cut, new issues don't have to yield as much as they previously did in order to beat inflation. And this is fine. The lower payments might infringe on our compounding strategy, but the true benefit of a long-term bond fund rises to the surface when interest rates are cut. It all comes down to the inverse relationship between a bond fund and the fed funds rate. If you're holding long-term bonds when interest rates go down, the bonds immediately have a higher resale value, all because of the length of time over which you've locked in those higher rates. So while cutting the fed funds rate will eventually reduce our interest payments, it immediately increases the value of our moderate- and long-term bond funds. The increase in the long-term fund will be the most profound.

Let's look at an example. The graph below compares three different Treasury funds between 2006 and 2018. This period is significant because it encompasses the financial crisis, when the fed funds rate was reduced to near-zero. The period is also subject to gradual increases in the fed funds rate that persisted for the next decade.

The funds compared are the iShares 1-3 Year Treasury Bond ETF (SHY), the iShares 7-10 Year Treasury Bond ETF (IEF), and the iShares 20+ Year Treasury Bond ETF (TLT).

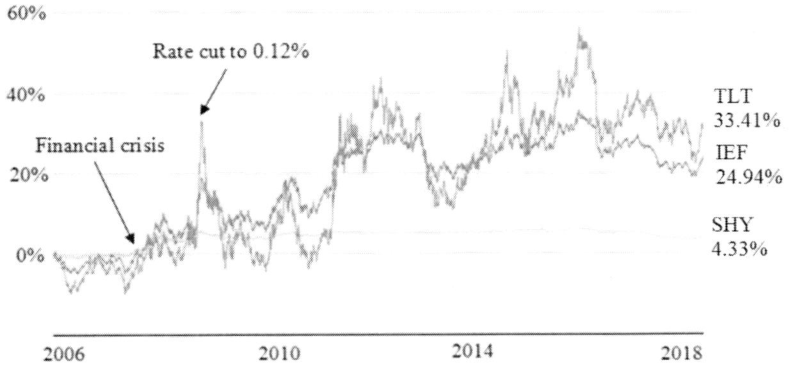

It's interesting to note that SHY, our one-to-three year holding, hardly budges. The fund did what it was intended to do. It pays a very modest interest rate premium and exhibits very little volatility. Our moderate- and long-term holdings fluctuated, as is expected. We see negative returns right off the bat, followed by gradual and steady increases, and then they spike as the fed funds rate is cut from a high of 5.34% to near-zero in an effort to stimulate the economy. It's significant that TLT, our twenty-plus-year holding, spikes higher than IEF, our seven-to-ten year holding. This is because the interest rates are locked in for greater durations.

As both funds fluctuate, TLT repeatedly moves higher and then lower than IEF. This is due to the inverse relationship between interest rates and bond value. Where IEF and TLT both pay interest rate premiums and fluctuate as the fed funds rate changes, SHY provides price stability.

What's especially interesting is that all three funds edged upwards at the start of the financial crisis. This is why we invest in bonds. They provide protection during economic downturns. But at the same time, we can't reliably time our bond fund investments according to changes in the economic environment. The volatility of the longer-term funds illustrates that losses can be incurred, all depending on when we get in and out. It's important not to view this as a market timing opportunity, just as it's important not to see bond funds as presenting undue risk. We simply need to understand how they function, and then take this into account as we allocate our portfolio and implement a rebalancing strategy. Given that we are only comparing bond funds, the chart appears more volatile than it truly is. A 33.41% gain is nothing to shake your head at, but when you consider that it was earned over a 12 year period, TLT has hardly budged. This is an illustration of the upside potential, and there will be times when bond funds go down in equal or greater proportions. The key is to diversify the portfolio across not only a variety of bond funds, including those with short durations, but as I keep emphasizing, diversify the portfolio across different markets. This will minimize not just the number of occurrences during which all of our holdings go down, but also the duration of time during which those occurrences last.

While stocks have always outperformed bonds over the long-run, there are many instances where bonds outperform stocks over two-to-five year periods. Bonds generally outperform stocks during recessions. When both interest rates and inflation are on the rise, short-term bonds are likely to outperform both stocks and long-term bonds.

Time is on our side as we build our portfolio, but the playing field will change when we reach retirement. At that point, it's no longer about beating inflation; it's about generating enough cash from your investments to live on. Bond funds will always fluctuate, but they're still perceived as safe compared to stocks and real estate. Preservation of capital becomes very important at retirement. If your portfolio takes a hit, you no longer have time to earn it back. So you'll want to increase your bond allocation as you age. When interest rates are cut to near-zero, the bond funds will again increase, and this aids in the preservation of capital. The only problem is that it will drastically reduce your income. We don't just want to insulate the portfolio against an economic downturn—*we need the interest payments to live on.* Once we reach retirement, beating inflation isn't as important as generating enough cash flow to live on. If we start with an average portfolio yield of 3.5% and rates are cut to 0.25% for an extended period of time, the total yield on our portfolio might fall to somewhere around 0.75%. We'll still be beating inflation by half a point, but our income will have been reduced by more than 4.5 times what it once was. This can significantly impair our retirement. In *Chapter 12: Rebalancing* we'll discuss ways to mitigate this type of situation. But before we get there, let's take a look at what happens when long-term Treasuries are in such high demand that the price is driven up, and the yield is resultantly driven so far down that they pay less than short-term bonds.

The phenomenon just described is known as an inverted yield curve. It's rare, but it is possible for long-term bonds to yield less than short-term bonds. It's a product of supply and demand that historically has corresponded with a pre-recessionary economic environment. The public perceives that interest rates are going to be cut, and this perception motivates investors to lock in long-term holdings out of concern that they won't be able to reinvest a short-term holding at a desirable rate. As demand for long-term holdings increases, the price goes up, and yield is driven down. If this persists to the point that a buyer would receive a higher yield on a short-term holding than on a long-term holding, an inverted yield curve is present.

Since 1970, an inverted yield curve *"has"* preceded every recession in the United States. And this leading economic indicator has provided investors with plenty of time to react. The shortest span between an inversion and the beginning of a recession is six months. The inversion occurred in June of 1973 and the corresponding recession began in December of 1973. The longest span before a financial crisis is seventeen months, with the inversion occurring in August of 2006 and the recession beginning in January of 2008. Yes, investors have plenty of time to react, but with recessions beginning anywhere from six to seventeen months after inversion, timing is still a challenge. My recommendation is to not react at all, but to simply follow through with the allocation strategy you put in place prior to the inversion. Allowing markets to work through their cycles provides the safest reward. When we attempt to time the market, we assume added risk in an effort to obtain a higher reward. And we accept the possibility that there will be no reward at all.

You may have noted my designation of the word *"has"* in the first sentence of the above paragraph. It's very easy to provide commentary on what the market *has* done. The history is there. All we need to do is look at it. Determining what the market *will* do is a different story. Prior to the financial crisis, the longest span between an inversion and a recession was fifteen months rather then seventeen. Yes, it's only a sixty day difference, but the market did something it hadn't done before. Who's to say that the next inverted yield curve won't come twenty months before the corresponding recession. And what guarantee is there that other events won't mitigate a recession. Perhaps we'll see an inversion take place sixty months before the next recession, with a second inversion occurring some forty-six months after the first. We can speculate as much as we want. We can also trade on the averages and hope that a pattern unfolds that conforms to past movements. A balanced portfolio that controls for risk removes both speculation and hope from the equation. We use bonds both to earn a distribution and to control for risk. But I do not recommend using them as a tool for speculation. When your long-term bond fund yields less than inflation, it's a short-term abnormality that will reverse. Building a well-diversified portfolio that's designed to weather a recession is a long-term plan that's been used by countless investors to accrue sustainable wealth. I recommend sustainability over speculation. And we'll see why in the coming chapters.

Corporate Bonds

Turning our attention to corporate bonds, it's important to note that there are both similarities and differences to Treasuries in the type of risk assumed. Both Treasuries and corporate bonds have interest rate risk. That's why long-term Treasuries pay a premium. Corporate bonds do the same. The longer the duration, the greater the premium. But corporate bonds come with a greater risk of default. Unlike our government, a corporation cannot back their bonds with taxing authority. And while we anticipate that the government will persist after each and every shutdown, corporations face different obstacles. They can file for bankruptcy in order to alleviate certain kinds of debt. Or they can shut their doors and liquidate. A benefit of holding debt over equity is that the interest payments are almost always required. The same doesn't apply to a dividend. Companies can cut their dividends at any time without consequence (aside from a hit to the stock price).

While required to make good on their obligations, companies (and governments too) can default. In the event that a company files for bankruptcy, the bondholder's rights take precedence over those of the shareholders. Debtors get paid before owners. And while a bondholder probably won't get their entire investment back during liquidation, getting paid before the shareholders does provide some consolation. Naturally, we're not buying bonds because of their liquidation rights. We buy them to control for risk. And we enjoy the cash flow they provide. But having liquidation rights that supersede other stakeholders is a nice benefit.

An additional risk that comes with corporate bonds is call risk. A call provision allows the issuer to repurchase and retire the bond. The issuer will exercise the call provision when interest rates are cut, as this prevents them from making payments that exceed the now lower market rate. This type of provision is designed to benefit the issuer at the expense of the investor. Should interest rates go up, the issuer will be content to keep making payments at the lower rate. The bondholder is left in a situation that is essentially lose-lose. When rates are cut, the issuer can call the bond, and the investor's next best option is to reinvest the funds in a newer issue with a smaller payment. Naturally, an investor won't purchase a bond with a call provision unless they are paid a premium. The premium will provide insulation when rates increase, but won't provide any protection when rates are cut and the call is exercised. Instead, most callable bonds come with a call protection, which is a clause that prevents the issuer from exercising the call until a certain amount of time has elapsed. This ensures that the investor earns at least some interest prior to the call being exercised. Other callable bonds come with a call price, which is a stated amount above par that the bondholder must be paid during a call. While a call is not in the bond holder's interest, they generally receive protection in one form or another.

Call provisions are not unique to corporate bonds. Any bond issue can include a call provision. But the U.S. Treasury has not released bonds with a call provision since 1984. For this reason, we will think of the call provision in terms of our corporate bond investments, and understand that our Treasury holdings will not be called.

The potential to earn more with corporate bonds is obvious. The investor will receive premiums for accepting both the default risk and the call risk (if applicable) that pertain to the specific issue. And just like Treasuries, there is also interest rate risk. In fact, a long duration doesn't just increase the interest rate risk, but also increases the period of time over which a bond can be called or go into default. The premiums will vary according to the issue, and the company's financial position will have a direct impact on the premium paid for the applicable risk factors. If company A is in a better financial position than company B, then company B will be forced to pay higher premiums. A host of factors impact the size of the premium, with the culmination of these factors influencing a rating that the bond receives from one of three agencies: Standard & Poor's, Moody's, and Fitch Group. The credit rating agencies have tremendous influence over the price of a bond. A bond rating of AAA to BBB- is considered investment grade, where a rating of BB+

to D is considered non-investment grade. The term "junk bonk" is attached to non-investment grade issues. Naturally, a junk bond will pay a higher premium than an investment grade bond. Depending on your appetite for risk, it's not necessary to avoid these bonds altogether. The yields are comparatively more attractive than those of investment grade bonds. By investing in an index fund the impact of individual issues going into default is mitigated, but the fund will be more volatile than other funds with similar duration. Additionally, junk bonds are prone to move in tandem with stocks, which differs from the movements of Treasuries and investment grade corporate bonds. This correlation should be considered when weighting the portfolio. A small junk bond allocation to accompany other bonds can serve as healthy diversification, while too much reliance on junk bonds will increase risk and fail to provide insulation when stocks decline. Each investor has varying preferences when it comes to risk, but if too much emphasis is placed on non-investment grade bonds, the impact is similar to what happens when the portfolio is weighted too heavily in favor of stocks.

Investment grade bonds should receive a larger allocation. A mix of both Treasury and corporate bond funds with varying maturities can be used to gain an edge over inflation, and also accelerate the benefits of compounding. I recommend limiting our exposure to junk bonds in the same manner that we limit our exposure to individual stocks. No more than 2.5% to 5% of the portfolio should be allocated to this type of debt. It will provide an extra bump in terms of yield, and some added diversification. A risk-averse investor who has 35% of their portfolio allocated to bonds might be inclined to hold 25% in Treasuries, 7.5% in investment grade corporate bonds, and 2.5% in junk bonds. A default risk premium is still earned on 10% of the portfolio, but a greater allocation forgoes the premium in favor of stability. All holdings with maturities greater than one year will be subject to interest rate risk, but this can still be mitigated by investing in funds with staggering maturities. Each fund presents its own unique characteristics in terms of risk and reward. And while each of the holdings is important, our concern isn't so much about how they behave individually, but about the impact they have on the portfolio when combined. By including some higher yielding bonds with additional risk, we increase our yield, but still maintain safety through diversification.

REITs

When most people start investing, they buy stocks. And when it comes to protecting those investments, they add a bond allocation to the portfolio. With the right approach, stocks and bonds can be combined to form a secure yet profitable portfolio. But far too many Americans take the wrong approach when it comes to real estate. The method described in *Dividend Investing* is no different from the method we'll use to invest in stocks and bonds. We're simply going to buy a fund (or several) that holds an index of REITs. The approach is simple, and it avoids the complexities that come with making a direct real estate acquisition. If you're a homeowner, then you understand the complexities I speak of. And while owning a home is manageable, building a diversified portfolio with direct real estate acquisitions is a full time job.

It's a mistake to consider yourself exposed to the real estate market simply because you own a home. Yes, your home is a big investment, and quite possibly the largest you'll ever make. There's nothing wrong with that. We need shelter, and by owning a home we not only obtain shelter, but also acquire an asset that will hopefully appreciate in value over the years. But when it comes to building a diversified portfolio that includes real estate, your house is not part of the equation. Your portfolio is separate and distinct from this investment. And while it's beneficial to own a home that increases in value, there's a good possibility that you'll want to retire in it, not because of it. Part of the problem boils down to the fact that homes don't pay any form of dividend (unless you rent out a room, or seek a reverse mortgage). But there are other disadvantages. For starters, it's incredibly difficult to diversify in the housing market, unless you're going to keep buying more homes. Most of us don't. What we own is a single home. And unlike an investment in a stock or bond fund, we can't sell a portion of it to reinvest in something else. It's an all or nothing exchange. And when you throw in property taxes, insurance, repairs, and all those other expenses that come with owning a home, it feels more like a liability than an asset. You might recognize a nice gain when you sell, but when you factor in all those expenses you'll incur throughout the years, it's quite possible that you won't come out as far ahead as you'd like.

But from an investment perspective there is one really nice advantage to owning a home. When it comes time to sell, the first $250,000 in gains is tax free so long as the home served as your primary residence during two of the previous five years. If you file a joint return, then they raise the exclusion to $500,000. As a taxpayer, there's really no reason to argue. Sometimes you have to take what Uncle Sam gives you, and this is a prime example of the tax code favoring the homebuyer over the stock investor.

It's nice to know that this break will be waiting for us down the road (so long as they don't change the tax code). But our goal is to build streams of dividend income that will support us through retirement, and while owning a home will prevent you from having to pay rent, it doesn't yield a dividend. As a security, your home is your very last resort in the event of a financial emergency. But it's much better to plan for those emergencies, and allow the home to serve the function that you intended it to serve.

What we truly want are real estate investments that pay rent, and when we invest in a REIT the rent is passed along in the form of a dividend. And these rental payments can be used in our compounding strategy just like any other dividend. That's what we're after. We want the rent to be passive income, something that's paid out as a dividend rather than worked for. If you were to buy a rental property, the income would be anything but passive. Landlords have a tough job. And when they get undesirable tenants, they really have their work cut out for them. There are companies that manage properties on the owner's behalf. It can be expensive, but it's a viable option, especially if you're investing in properties outside of your city or state. If you ever decide to invest in a vacation rental, do yourself a favor and study the tax benefits thoroughly. There are some tremendous breaks to owning this type of investment, so long as you structure your personal use of the property strategically. And those rental payments will function just like any other form of passive income.

From a portfolio construction perspective, what we're really looking for is diversification. We want a sustainable stream of rental payments, but we want to obtain this without the value of our holdings tied to a specific neighborhood or tourist destination. Just like the other asset classes, an index fund is an easy way to gain broad market exposure. Instead of holding stocks or bonds, we'll want to invest in an index of real estate investment trusts, or REITs.

A REIT is a company that owns and operates income-producing properties. This includes apartments and vacation rentals. It also includes hospitals, shopping centers, hotels, resorts, office space, and many other types of properties. While a single REIT can own many properties, you'll be in a better position if you buy an index of REITs. The strategy is similar to owning an index of stocks. A single REIT can be mismanaged, but an index of REITs will offset the impact of a single company.

There's nothing wrong with investing in individual REITs if you know what you're doing. Given that the risk involved with holding an individual REIT is similar to that of holding an individual stock, you'll again want to be conservative with your allocations. But if you've already allocated 2.5% to 5% of your portfolio to individual stock selections, then I won't recommend taking the same approach with real estate. For starters, 10% of the portfolio is way too much to have invested in individual selections, even if those selections are pulled from two different markets. It might be feasible in the early stages, but as the portfolio gets bigger it puts too much capital at risk. Additionally, you don't want to invest in more individual holdings than you can monitor. If you're devoting time to stocks, it's best to focus exclusively on stocks. If you want to follow REITs, it's best to focus exclusively on REITs. Even professional analysts who dedicate themselves full-time to a particular segment or batch of securities have limitations. The self-directed investor who comes home from work ready to monitor their holdings will face even larger time constraints. There's definitely an advantage to being specialized. So if you prefer following REITs over stocks, then go ahead and specialize in REITs. There are intricacies to investing in REITs that are well beyond the scope of

Dividend Investing. But like anything else, it's a skill that can be developed.

One of the intricacies you'll find is that during periods of high inflation, REITs are prone to outperform stocks. Another intricacy is that REITs are required to distribute their rents. And this is a huge advantage over investing in stocks. While a company isn't required to pay any form of dividend unless they choose to, REITs are required to distribute at least 90% of their income to the shareholders. This is great for compounding, as well as generating cash flow in retirement. And you don't need to invest in individual REITs to take advantage of these intricacies. You'll get the same benefits through an index fund.

When it comes to selecting your funds, it's important to note that there are two kinds of REITs: equity REITs and mortgage REITs. Equity REITs are the most common, and as the name implies, investors receive an ownership interest in the underlying properties. With a mortgage REIT, you're investing in some combination of residential and commercial mortgages. The purpose of the mortgage REIT is to provide liquidity to the real estate market, and this also provides investors with an opportunity to build a stream of dividend income. Both equity REITs and mortgage REITs are required to distribute 90% of their income to the shareholders. And while both types of REITs are known for offering attractive yields, the yield on a mortgage REIT can be substantially higher, oftentimes reaching into the double digits.

The entire point in structuring the portfolio around different asset classes is to ensure that you're not just diversified within a market, but that you're also diversified across markets. That way an economic event that negatively impacts the entire real estate market won't take a toll on your entire portfolio.

Mortgage REITs provide an opportunity to earn strong yields, but they come with additional risk. And when we view the mortgage REIT in terms of the greater portfolio, we see that they function in the exact same manner as the other debt instruments that we'll be investing in. Even though the mortgage REIT is classified as real estate, its behavior will mimic that of our bond holdings. The similarities are so strong that it's best to limit our exposure to mortgage REITs in the same way we would with junk bonds.

For starters, the value of a mortgage REIT is inversely related to the fed funds rate. When the interest rate rises, the value of a mortgage REIT declines. And when the interest rate gets cut, the value of a mortgage REIT increases. There's also default risk involved, as history has shown that not every homeowner pays their mortgage. And even when mortgages are packaged together in tranches, history has also shown us that certain economic conditions can cause defaults to spike. There is some protection, of course. Just like in the bond market where a Treasury is viewed as safe in terms of default, mortgages that are backed by a government agency, such as Fannie Mae, Freddie Mac, or Ginnie Mae, are perceived to have very low default risk. A private entity, on the other and, is at liberty to issue mortgage-backed securities that are not backed by the U.S. Government. So by restricting our investments to mortgage REITs that are backed by a government agency we can, to an extent, control for default risk. And just like bonds, the greater the risk of default, the greater the premium that must be paid.

An additional risk is that of early payment. When interest rates decline, homeowners have an added incentive to pay off their mortgage. It makes sense, because no one wants to pay more than the going rate. Provisions that allow homeowners to pay their mortgage early essentially function as a call provision. And just like with a bond, the investor should be paid a premium for investing in a security that's prone to this type of risk.

As we structure our portfolios, a mortgage REIT should be treated as a bond rather than a real estate investment, and it should be treated as a risky one at that. Above, I indicate that junk bonds can be used in small increments to get some added yield while increasing diversification. A mortgage REIT can be used in the same way. But this investment should not be made in addition to junk bonds, but rather should be made in place of or in conjunction with your junk bond allocation. Both investments are risky. Combined, they should account for no more than 5% of the total portfolio. The fact that some mortgage REITs are backed by government agencies is a strong argument for favoring this type of investment over an allocation to junk bonds. The often-times higher dividend yield further strengthens the argument. The benefit to holding a separate fund for each type of debt instrument is that they don't always move in tandem. When interest rates change, their movements will be highly correlated, and this overrides the benefits of diversifying. Conversely, an event that causes corporations to default on their debt won't necessarily cause homeowners to stop paying their mortgages. So there is an advantage to holding both junk bonds and mortgage REITs, though it's still recommended that the combined allocation be small.

When it comes to equity REITs, we're going to treat these exactly as they are—*this is your chance to invest in actual real estate, not a debt obligation*. An equity REIT holds physical properties that, in the event of liquidation, have greater value than debt instruments. They do not function like bonds, and in most market conditions they will not behave the same as stocks. Unlike a mortgage REIT, this provides the cross-market diversification that we seek. And the opportunity to earn strong dividend yields is ripe.

Consistent with our other investments, we'll want to acquire index funds that provide broad market exposure to equity REITs at the lowest possible cost. Early on, a fund that represents the entire domestic real estate market will be sufficient. But as the portfolio grows, certain funds can be added to hone in exclusively on residential real estate or specific business properties, such as retail, office space, healthcare, and tourist destinations. Just as the stock investor can benefit from specializing in a specific segment, so too can the REIT investor. But I again want to emphasize that the point of specialization is to get an edge over the market because you're knowledgeable of a specific segment. The broader the specialization, the lower the rate of success. If real estate is not your area of expertise, a broad market index fund is sufficient.

It's important to note that some indexes will combine both equity and mortgage REITs. Even a fund that tracks an index that strictly follows equity REITs will state in their prospectus that they invest "substantially all" of their assets in securities that make up the underlying index. The remainder of the assets might be invested in a short-term debt instrument, and a portion might even be allocated to a mortgage REIT. The goal is not to scour the holdings of every fund we buy in order to pinpoint a handful extraneous investments. If 90% of a fund's assets are invested in the underlying index and the fund is offered at a low cost, then it's suitable for our needs. It's unlikely that any other holdings present in the fund will be outliers in terms of risk, though it's not entirely impossible. Most funds are simply aiming for a safe return on their idle cash.

But let's suppose a fund that tracks an equity REIT does invest idle cash in securities that are riskier than those that make up the underlying index. Because of our investment strategy we'll be invested in three different asset classes, so conceivably one-third of the portfolio might be invested in a single equity REIT fund. If the fund invests 90% of its assets in the underlying index and the remaining 10% in a combination of mortgage REITs and junk bonds, then this will constitute 3.3% of the entire portfolio (33.33 x 0.1 = 3.3%). This is in line with the percent of the portfolio that we should feel comfortable investing in high risk, high reward assets, though it's possible that we've already made these investments ourselves.

As a rule of thumb, the financial world is not going to provide a service without charging for it. If the management fees are low and in line with a passive investment strategy, the chances of a fund manager going after above-market returns rather than earning a bit of interest on idle cash is extremely low. As your portfolio gets bigger, and your need to diversify further within each asset class increases, the benefits of tracking how idle cash is invested gets smaller and smaller.

You might start off with a single equity REIT fund that provides broad market exposure to the domestic real estate market. If you believe that healthcare facilities have a favorable outlook, you might eventually add a fund that tracks healthcare REITs. As time passes and the portfolio gets bigger, you might even add a couple funds that track foreign real estate markets, perhaps one invested in various emerging markets, and another that invests in developed

European countries. If you're allocating 30% of your entire portfolio to real estate, you could then leave 22.5% in the broad market domestic fund that you started off with, and allocate 2.5% of the portfolio to each of the other three funds. As we seek higher returns, we assume greater risk, and the recommended approach is to do so conservatively. A risk tolerant investor might allocate a higher proportion of the portfolio to emerging markets. And the allocation made to European countries might be deemed as only a touch riskier than investing in domestic real estate. Different investors will take different approaches to combining their asset classes. And that's fine. The approach advocated in *Dividend Investing* is to invest the majority of the portfolio in domestic markets that have a history of always beating inflation over the long-run, and then attempt to gain an edge over these markets by investing conservative portions of the portfolio in riskier segments.

Foreign markets are an excellent way to chase higher returns while also increasing your diversification. But when it comes to emerging markets, it pays to be conservative. A country that is still developing can provide higher returns when times are good, but will face harder struggles during an economic downturn. I prefer to diversify into developed countries because they are in a position to offer higher dividends, but from a growth perspective, emerging markets are an excellent tool for increasing the size of the pie that dividends are going to be paid from. Let's take a closer look at foreign markets, not just in terms of real estate, but in terms of all three of the asset classes that we'll be investing in.

Foreign Markets

As we move closer and closer to retirement, diversification becomes increasingly more important. At the beginning it's okay to hold just a few funds that are not only geared towards growth, but also provide at least a modest amount of dividend income for the purpose of compounding. As we move closer to retirement, we not only want to increase our dividend distributions, but also want to keep the capital that we've accumulated safe. We do this in two ways: (1) increasing our bond allocation each year, and (2) making sure the portfolio is properly diversified.

Foreign markets provide an excellent opportunity to increase diversification. A portfolio that has exposure to the domestic stock, bond, and real estate markets can easily add foreign holdings for each asset class. It's as simple as finding a low fee index fund that covers the region of interest, and then adding it to the portfolio. When the U.S. stock market takes a slump, we now have more than just the domestic bond and real estate markets to pick up the slack. Perhaps the emerging markets are taking off. Or maybe things look good in Asia. At the same time, these foreign markets could slump when domestic markets accelerate. And, of course, the worst case scenario is that we enter into a global slump. Like anything else, we want to contain our exposure so that no single market drives the portfolio. By increasing the number of markets that we're invested in, we decrease the chance that all of our holdings will enter correction territory simultaneously. Diversification provides protection. But when it comes to foreign markets the investor needs to understand the risks involved.

Just like the bond investor who demands a premium for accepting additional risk, the foreign market investor also requires a premium. Most notably, when investing in foreign markets there's an exchange rate risk. When invested in securities that are not only denominated in a foreign currency, but also pay distributions in that currency, there's a risk that the U.S dollar will strengthen. If the U.S. dollar keeps going up, then dividends that need to be converted from a foreign currency into a progressively strengthening dollar will keep getting smaller and smaller. At the same time, if the dollar gets weaker, then the process of converting your dividends to U.S. dollars will yield more income rather than less. The dividend is a good example because it's a recurring distribution that is vulnerable to fluctuations in the exchange rate. The change might work in your favor, or it might not. But more than just the dividend is exposed to this risk. There's also a currency exchange when you buy the stock, and again when you sell the stock. Though you may have purchased the stock because of the company's outlook for growth, changes in the exchange rate will influence the size of the gain or loss you incur.

At the same time, companies expose themselves to exchange rate risk any time they do business across borders, and this will impact the earnings they report. Both your domestic and foreign holdings are susceptible to this risk. If a large U.S. company has operations in Europe, they will do business in the Euro and then translate their earnings into U.S. dollars to report them on the financial statements. In this respect, an investor who buys a holding in a domestic broad market index fund is accepting foreign exchange rate risk, though the risk is quite small. If instead the investor were to buy a single U.S. company with large foreign operations, they would find themselves more exposed to fluctuations in the value of the U.S. dollar. The risk is more profound when the investor enters directly into a foreign market, even if done by means of an index fund. Instead of the fund holding domestic companies with some foreign operations, the operations are now predominately foreign.

There's also increased risk when it comes to tariffs. No investor is ever completely free from this risk. A tariff enacted here in the U.S. could negatively impact a domestic industry, even though the tariff is aimed at a foreign country. And a tariff that penalizes one country may very well benefit another. Or it could just move production back to the U.S. While this risk is always prevalent, it increases when we invest in foreign markets.

As we gain greater exposure to foreign markets, the impact of exchange rates and tariffs increases. The more narrow the exposure, the more volatile the investment. And if the exposure is too broad, the benefits of diversification are lost. Whether diversification is achieved through foreign markets or a different approach, holding too many funds in the portfolio will decrease the returns. If funds are spread across too many markets, the winners don't truly stand out.

Foreign exposure is great for the portfolio. But the exposure should not be applied to all three asset classes. Exchange rate risk will move the price of a stock in the same direction that it moves the price of a bond or piece of real estate. And we only need moderate exposure to this type of risk. Similarly, an emerging market that exhibits exponential growth should deliver strong gains in both the stock and real estate markets. So if it's desirable to gain exposure to markets in both the European Union and the Asia-Pacific regions, it's not necessary, or even beneficial, to hold stocks, bonds, and real estate in both of these markets. A more efficient approach would be to invest in a stock fund for one region, and a real estate fund for the other. With the exception of a default risk premium, there's little to be gained from foreign exposure to bonds, because when the market outperforms it's the stocks and real estate that increase in value. Bonds will simply continue to pay the interest that they're supposed to pay. They should be avoided during your working years, but modest exposure could provide some benefit in retirement. As you begin to rely more heavily on fixed income you might want to decrease or eliminate your foreign equity holdings in favor of a global bond fund.

When we get to the tax section we'll see that the dividend investor is penalized for receiving dividends from certain foreign corporations. Most stock dividends are taxed at a preferential rate of 15%. A foreign corporation must meet certain requirements in order for their dividends to receive the same treatment, but most foreign corporations that trade on an established U.S. stock exchange will qualify. When investing in an index fund, however, exposure increases, as does the likelihood that at least part of the dividends received will not qualify for preferential tax treatment. And there will be similar considerations when it comes to bonds and real estate.

Chapter 11

Asset Allocation

Asset allocation is the cornerstone of a successful investment strategy. That's why I've alluded to it more than a dozen times so far. And for the remainder of the book I'll continue to reiterate the content of this chapter and how it relates to other material. It's really that important. Any long-term success you achieve without a conscious effort to diversify your investments and then gradually shift over to safer markets as you progress through your investment career—*that is, any long-term success you achieve without proper asset allocation*—is likely attributable only to luck. Many investors argue that asset allocation is in fact *the* most important component to investing. And while I acknowledge the validity of the argument, I'm going to propose that asset allocation gets second place, right behind the amount of money saved—*after all, there's nothing to allocate if you don't fund your portfolio.* This is true not just for the dividend investor, but for all investors. It takes sacrifice to fund the portfolio, so we want to make sure those hard earned (*and painfully saved*) dollars are invested wisely. It's important not just to recognize the risks and rewards that are present in different markets, but to understand that risk can be reduced, and rewards can be maintained, as different markets are combined in various proportions. An allocation to bonds will add safety to a portfolio that also invests in stocks. Bonds will also reduce long-term returns if added too aggressively early in the investment horizon, but they can also save a portfolio from disaster when the investor no longer has enough time to recover from a stock market crash. The ultimate goal is to combine assets in such a way so that you reap the largest possible reward for your tolerated level of risk.

As dividend investors our focus has been and will continue to be on stocks, bonds, and real estate. These are the markets that pay "dividends" in one form or another. But other investors might allocate a portion of their portfolio to commodities. Gold is a common hedge against inflation. Some investors like to hold foreign currency, while others dabble in collectibles and fine art. And while profitable investments can be churned from all kinds of markets, we're only going to focus on markets that pay a dividend.

Before we get carried away with our dividends, let's define asset allocation and take a closer look at its workings. According to Investopedia, asset allocation is an investment strategy that aims to balance risk and reward by apportioning a portfolio's assets according to an individual's goals, risk tolerance, and investment horizon. The three main asset classes—*equities, fixed-income, and cash and cash equivalents*—have different levels of risk and return, so each will behave differently over time.

We've already discussed equities and fixed income. And we know that we can earn a distribution from these holdings. This is all we need to form a diversified portfolio. While cash and cash equivalents are important, we won't rely too heavily on any asset class that isn't expected to beat inflation over the long-haul. Money market accounts are great for earning at least a little bit on cash that needs to remain liquid, but the longer you leave money in one of these accounts, the greater the probability that the purchasing power of your savings will erode.

It's important to have a cash reserve in the event of a job loss or other halt to your income, but we're not going to treat it as a component of the portfolio. This is cash that you're sitting on, not investing. Cash should always earn at least the going money market rate and be more liquid than a CD, and the interest payments should always be compounded. We know that the appreciation of our cash reserve won't keep pace with inflation, but we can still compound the interest earned at the money market rate. And we've already seen what just a small compounded return can add up to over an extended period of time. Even though the purchasing power is expected to decline, we still want whatever return we can get while the funds remain liquid. And for what it's worth, I truly hope that you never have to eat into your cash reserve. If the cash reserve simply sits idle while the interest compounds for thirty-plus years, it will be good for both your emotional health and your financial health. On top of that, you'll have more money to invest with over your lifetime if you never have to go through the trouble of replenishing your cash reserve.

If you do keep idle cash in the portfolio, consider it part of the 2.5% to 5% that can be allocated to individual stock selections. When stocks are over priced, hold cash. And when bargains can be found, buy stocks. This is a conservative approach at timing the market. But our ultimate goal is to achieve the largest return possible while controlling our tolerance for risk.

By "tolerance for risk" I'm referring to one's willingness to take on riskier investments in an effort to achieve higher returns. It's different for everyone, and much of the tolerance pertains to one's capacity to see things through during a recession. Generally speaking, the higher the risk the greater the reward. But there's a huge difference between taking on so much risk that you guarantee your own failure and upping the level of risk to something appropriate for your personality, age, and financial situation. If you're going to get scared and sell your assets after they've dropped in value, then you need to allocate the majority of your portfolio into risk free Treasury notes or bonds and only assume minor exposure to equities, real estate, and other types of bonds. Your returns won't be impressive, but you'll never have to watch your portfolio cycle through a downturn.

If you're the type of person who doesn't even bother logging into your brokerage account during a recession because you have confidence that the market will bounce back, then you should weight the portfolio more heavily towards equities as you minimize your exposure to Treasuries. There are literally hundreds of variations between these two extremes, just as there are literally hundreds of subclasses that we can hold within each of our asset classes. *It's going to be fun! And you're going to make money!* But you need to maintain an appropriate asset allocation, not just for your personality type, but also for your age. The weight of your different holdings should change as you progress through the investment horizon.

It's important to recognize that stocks and real estate keep getting lumped together in terms of risk, yet our allocation to Treasuries is thought to be risk free. This doesn't mean that stocks and real estate always behave the same way at all times. In fact, we really don't want them to. It's to our advantage if they move in opposite directions at least some of the time, as this will have an offsetting impact on portfolio volatility. The fact that real estate tends to beat stocks during periods of inflation, but does worse than stocks during periods of disinflation, means that the two asset classes will serve as good compliments within the portfolio.

Growth is important early on, but the closer we get to retirement, the more stable we want the portfolio to be. And while it's impossible to always earn large capital gains, by controlling for risk we can strive to earn modest yet steady capital gains as we collect our dividends. There will be times when different asset classes move in unison, and this means that there will be times when both stocks and real estate decline in value. The great recession of 2007-2008 is an obvious example, and it illustrates why we need to treat both stocks and real estate as risky, while Treasuries provide a haven for safe yet limited returns.

If you've been working with a financial advisor, try to remember if he ever had you complete a questionnaire to determine your tolerance for risk. A good financial advisor will start with this evaluation and use it to determine how much of your portfolio to allocate amongst the different asset classes. This is preferred over the financial advisor who claims their firm has "experts" on hand to select the right stocks and mutual funds for their clients. In fact, the very best financial advisors will offer what is called a fiduciary responsibility, meaning that they agree to act in your best interest. The overwhelming majority of fiduciary advisors use an investment approach that relies on broad market exposure to different asset classes in the proper proportions. They provide advice based on the concepts discussed in this chapter. And they typically charge a fee based on the size of your portfolio, rather than charging a commission every time you incur a trade. This is ideal because it aligns their goals with yours. Your advisor maximizes his pay by maximizing the size of your portfolio, rather than increasing his commissions by recommending trades that you don't really need to make. You should only work with a financial advisor who is willing to assume a fiduciary responsibility.

While risk tolerance is indeed different for every investor, our goal is to build wealth from which we will earn dividends for the rest of our lives. The capital dedicated to this endeavor should be significant, and over time we should make changes to our risk tolerance to ensure that our accumulated wealth is safe. The questionnaire discussed above is a good start. If you're not working with an advisor it's easy to find one online and assess your own tolerance for risk. Nobody knows you better than yourself, including your financial advisor. And while a questionnaire is helpful, you might already have a pretty good feel for the amount of risk that you're willing to endure.

If you are investing through a discount broker there is a huge advantage to just keeping things simple. In lieu of the questionnaire, a well-recognized rule of thumb is to own your age in bonds. If you start your portfolio at age 25, then 25% of your investments should be allocated to bonds and 75% divided between stocks and real estate. By the time you reach age 35 you should then have 35% allocated to bonds and 65% divided between socks and real estate. The part allocated to bonds is predetermined for each year, but how you divide the remainder between stocks and real estate is a matter of personal preference.

Many financial advisors suggest this approach, but I'm going to say that this rule of thumb is a tad too conservative. At age 25 you could have upwards of 40 years until retirement, and allocating a quarter of your portfolio to a low return investment like bonds is certain to stunt your growth. In fact, most investors express a greater willingness for risk when they have not been through a bear market, as would most likely be the case at the beginning of your investment career. So I'm going to recommend that you embrace risk when you first start out, and go chase after those high returns. When a bear comes along you should embrace it too, and not let your first experience with a market pullback prevent you from following through with your allocation strategy.

Your twenties is the safest time for you to accept risk. You should go all in with the risky investments. Your portfolio is likely still small, so there isn't a lot of capital at risk, and you have the rest of your life to earn back any losses. So you might as well buy up as many stock and real estate shares as you can, and let the older investors buy up some bonds on their way to the golf course. Early in life you'll be working hard for your money, so make sure your money is also working hard for you. Once you reach 30 you can start toning things down, but just a little at first. My recommendation is to own your age less 10 years in bonds (rather than simply owning your age in bonds). To me, it just doesn't make sense to start investing in bonds before you turn 30.

If you're properly allocated there is never a reason to be afraid of a bear market, even if you're young and assuming a high allocation to stocks and real estate. We already know that a bear market is your best friend during the early years. You have relatively little to lose and the long-term dividend yield on investments purchased during a bear market will reach astronomical proportions as you progress through life. But if 25%+ of your portfolio is allocated to bonds, the benefits of a bear market will be diminished. As you proceed to dollar cost average each month or quarter, a good chunk of your contribution will go into bonds instead of buying stocks at discount prices. Even if stocks are doing well when you start out, it's likely that you'll see a bear market at some point in your twenties. And if you don't, all the more reason to be heavily invested in stocks and real estate. At this age it truly is a win-win situation. If markets go down you will harvest some great dividend yields to last the rest of your life. If they go up, then you'll sacrifice good dividend yields for some healthy capital gains. Under either scenario, you'll want to start reducing risk as you enter your thirties, and allocating just 20% of your portfolio to risk free bonds is a good place to start.

By age 30 you've likely accumulated something worth protecting, but if you protect too much then you're again stunting your growth. Even when stocks look expensive, markets can continue to rise indefinitely, and it's impossible to predict exactly when they will reverse. A bear market isn't nearly as friendly in your thirties as it is in your twenties, but it's still more beneficial than hitting one in your forties or fifties. New capital still has plenty of time to grow if thrown at a bear market in your thirties. In fact, we'll continue dollar cost averaging right up until our sixties; it's just that we're going to adjust our tolerance for risk along the way.

The investment game is very different once you've amassed some wealth. A bear market still provides plenty of discounts to throw new capital at, but once you've built up your portfolio the bear will also take a great big bite out of your existing investments. And this is precisely why we want to cross over into bonds, albeit gradually, because proper asset allocation allows the long-term investor to benefit from both bull and bear markets without having to predict market direction. After age 30, the 20%+ of your portfolio that is now allocated to bonds is presumably protected from the bear, which creates an opportunity to reallocate a portion of these funds back into riskier investments after the bear has eaten away at the price. Again, we're not attempting to predict market direction. We don't want to sell the entire 20%+ bond allocation and buy equities. That would be too risky. So once the bear arrives, we need a systematic process that will help us reallocate from bonds into stocks in a safe and beneficial manner. We'll discuss the best way to do this in just a bit, but here's a tiny hint that you probably saw coming a mile away—*it's called rebalancing!*

As you move into your forties and fifties you should start allocating 30%+ and 40%+, respectively, of your portfolio to bonds, with the majority of this allocation going into risk free Treasuries. By this point you should know exactly what a bear market looks like, have experienced the benefits of not only seeing the bear through, but of dollar cost averaging into larger holdings while prices are low. Your wealth should be shaping up to something sizeable, and it's very possible that you wouldn't be able to earn this wealth back in its entirety if you lose some of your capital this late in life. At the same time, you're still looking at somewhere between 15 to 25 years until retirement, and growth should still be a factor, albeit a less important factor. You've proven to yourself that you have the intestinal fortitude to survive a bear market. And just as you saw in your thirties when only 20%+ of your portfolio was allocated to bonds, having 30%+ to 40%+ of your holdings in a risk free asset class is like having cash on hand just waiting for the next crash.

This might sound scary, especially as you get older. Selling large chunks of your Treasuries in order to throw some cash at an equity market that's just been ripped to shreds might even seem barbaric. But if you follow the strategy outlined in the following pages, it's all very rational. It should be carried out in a very stoic and civilized manner. The very practice of taking gains as you scoop up discounts from opposing markets should become second nature. The key, again, is to see the bear through and to always do what you told yourself you were going to do before the bear arrived.

A lot of financial advisors truly earn their pay during bear markets. This is when they receive the most phone calls. They have frantic customers who are scared and want to sell everything at the worst possible time. And the good ones do a lot of hand-holding for their customers; *it's not an easy job*. If you, as a self-directed investor, are likely to sell when things get scary, then an advisor might be worth the fee (so long as you pick the right advisor).

So far we've discussed what asset allocation is. We've gone over the types of markets we want to invest in. We know that we'll need to determine our tolerance for risk in order to allocate the right amount of money to each of these markets. We've touched on the advantages (and disadvantages) of doing this with a financial advisor. We understand to some extent that we don't always want our investments to move in the same direction at the same time. And whatever happens, we don't ever want to get scared and sell the middle of a bear market (as this will completely destroy the portfolio).

But how exactly do we determine our asset allocation? What's this rebalancing thing all about? Will it really force us to buy low and sell high without having to predict market direction? And if so, how does it all work?

The simplest answer is that it all comes down to correlation. Do the assets we've invested in move in the same or different directions under various market conditions? And how exactly does this all happen?

Essentially, we want to invest in different assets that do not exhibit a high degree of positive correlation. Positive correlation is when different assets move in the same direction at the same time. They don't necessarily need to be moving at the same pace, just in the same direction. One asset can be going up faster than another, but if they are both moving in an upward trend then they are said to be positively correlated. The same terminology applies when different assets trend downward at the same time. The more time they spend moving in the same direction, the stronger the correlation. If they have a history of only moving in the same direction during very specific, or even random, intervals, then the correlation is said to be weak, though it's still positive if the times during which they behave the same exceed the times during which they don't. It's also worth noting that correlation is not static. Two assets can exhibit a high degree of positive correlation for an extended period of time, but this can change, and market factors may force them to stop exhibiting any correlation at all.

Correlation can be measured in statistical terms on a scale from -1 to +1, with -1 signifying perfect negative correlation and +1 signifying perfect positive correlation. In the middle of these ranges is non-correlation, which is measured on a scale of -0.3 to +0.3. So anything between -1 and -0.3 exhibits negative correlation. Assets measured between -0.3 to +0.3 are said to not be correlated. And anything above +0.3 is said to be positively correlated.

Markets are not capable of exhibiting completely negative correlation (-1). But if they were, this *might* be good for the dividend investor. It would mean that as one market class goes down, another goes up by the exact same amount. So if you invest in both markets, your holdings will not only maintain their value, they will also distribute dividends as they do so. Thus, if asset A drops by 10% while yielding a dividend of 3.5%, and asset B increases by 10% while also yielding 3.5%, your portfolio will provide consistent returns of 3.5%. In reality, this type of perfectly negative correlation is not achievable, and when we look at how capital gains should be used to grow our portfolio, and thus increase the size of the pie that dividends are distributed from, it's not even desirable. Theoretically, perfect negative correlation could be accomplished by shorting a security while simultaneously taking a long position, but there's really no point in doing this. The net result is negative because you'll owe back any dividends earned on the borrowed shares, and fees, commissions, and taxes will chomp away at whatever dividend income you do get out of your long position.

Just like market timing, short selling is not something I recommend. As we discussed in *Chapter 6: Attributes to Consider When Selecting Stocks*, short selling is the equivalent of profiting from a company's misfortune rather than investing in one that you think will be successful. It's not a tool that should be used by retirement investors. Our goal is to make money while keeping things simple. All you need to do is save, dollar cost average, reinvest your dividends, allocate appropriately, and rebalance your portfolio. These are simple concepts to master, and they are key to securing a safe yet plentiful retirement.

As far as correlation is concerned, we likely won't include any assets in the portfolio that are negatively correlated, even if the correlation is closer to -0.3. If two markets are negatively correlated it means that more often than not they will be moving in different directions. This is good from a safety perspective. As one asset goes down, another goes up, and this hedges our bets as the dividend income comes rolling in. But we've already seen what growth can do for a portfolio, and we know that the bigger the pie the bigger the dividend distribution. We're long-term investors, and that means we only want to invest in assets that have a history of beating inflation over extended periods of time. It's extremely difficult to find two asset classes that are both going to beat inflation over periods of 20 to 40 years, yet will move in opposite directions more often than they move in the same direction. So what we really want are asset classes that will not only beat inflation, but do not exhibit any correlation (the ones measured between -0.3 +0.3). And when this cannot be achieved, we will settle for assets that are positively correlated, yet exhibit a weak correlation (the ones that are measured above +0.3, but no where near +1).

By diversifying our portfolio into funds that do not exhibit strong positive correlation, we not only minimize the size of a decline in our portfolio, but also minimize the duration of time during which the portfolio stays in the red. This provides safety against both short- and long-term downturns.

What we truly want to avoid is investing in assets that exhibit strong positive correlation, meaning that their values are affected by the same types of events and therefore spend long durations of time moving in tandem. There's little benefit to combining these assets. For example, if we invest in 100 different banks, the portfolio should not be considered diversified just because 100 is a large number. There are market conditions that will affect all banks in either a positive or negative manner. Each bank is susceptible to other movements predicated purely on how well the bank performs relative to its competition, but this will never change the fact that certain economic events (such as a change in interest rates) affects all banks simultaneously. All

100 stocks will exhibit strong positive correlation, and it would be much safer to diversify into a variety of different market sectors.

If market correlation is a new concept then it might feel very theoretical at this point, and the applicability may not yet be obvious. Let's review a very simple scenario and then extrapolate how this might be applied to broad market movements. To start, let's take two companies, one that makes ice cream and one that makes hot chocolate.

In the summer ice cream sales are booming. This makes the ice cream company more profitable than it was in the preceding months, and the stock price will increase. In the winter, the ice cream company will face a massive decline in sales, and this will happen just as the hot chocolate company experiences a huge increase in sales. This will cause the value of the ice cream company's stock to decline just as the hot chocolate company's stock takes off. These stocks are said to be negatively correlated because they move in different directions. Perfect negative correlation, as we've stated, is impossible to achieve. There will always be instances where assets of any type display at least some level of positive correlation. And the nature of correlation will change with time. Stocks that once exhibited negative correlation can become positively correlated. A perfect example is during a deep recession. Investors will get scared and sell both their ice cream and hot chocolate stocks at the same time. When a recession hits it doesn't matter what the weather is like. People are scared and have a need for liquidity, so it increases the probability that they will sell shares of both companies. When this happens the stocks will move in tandem, even if they don't move at the exact same pace. At times, investor sentiment can serve as a much stronger force than true economic conditions. Does the investor with a 20 year investment horizon care if it's winter or summer when they make their investments? Over this time span, seasons become trivial and other factors will determine whether the investor prefers the ice cream market over the hot chocolate market.

In practice, the entire example is an oversimplification because most packaged food companies make a variety of products. In all likelihood the ice cream you enjoyed last night was made by a company that also produces the hot chocolate you'll consume this coming winter. The time of year should have very little impact on the price of a packaged food company's stock—*people tend to eat all year long*.

The point I want to instill is that negative correlation is not required in order to reduce risk. As long as we hold a variety of assets that do not exhibit strong positive correlation, risk reduction is achieved. The best way to do this is to hold both stocks and bonds. Real estate is another nice addition. And when we throw foreign markets into the mix, further opportunities to diversify into funds that at worst are only minimally correlated will abound.

When stocks tank, we want to see our bonds edge up so the entire portfolio doesn't have to be dragged through the mud. When real estate is on fire, it's okay if stocks are only doing so-so. When they cut the fed funds rate it could give the value of our long-term bond fund a healthy jolt, but the need to cut the rate is also an indication that other markets are suffering. The overarching goal is to minimize the impact of market downturns by holding other markets that simultaneously prosper. And if all markets pay a distribution of some sort, be it a dividend, rent, or interest payment, then the portfolio will increase in value as losses are averaged out against gains. But the benefits don't stop there. If we implement a consistent rebalancing strategy, then we're not simply talking about losses being averaged out against gains. We're talking about gains being recognized while our losing assets serve as discount material for further investment. The benefits of rebalancing are strong. And when we combine this approach with a variety of markets that will beat inflation over the long-run, the impact multiplies. It's just like the benefit of compounding our dividends over an extended period of time. And there's no reason why we can't implement both of these strategies simultaneously.

Chapter 12

Rebalancing

We're finally here, the chapter of the book where we see how a rebalancing strategy can assist us in (*almost*) always recognizing gains instead of losses. The bedrock, of course, is finding markets that have a history of beating inflation over the long-run, do not exhibit high positive correlation, and then determining the percent of the portfolio we want to invest in each of these markets. Risk tolerance is different for everyone, but we'll proceed as though the right mix is what we discussed above, your age minus 10 years allocated to bonds, with the remainder divided between stocks and real estate. In the following examples we'll assume equal holdings in both stocks and real estate, but in practice the allocation could be very different.

We'll start by keeping things simple. In the first example we're only going to invest in one bond fund, one stock fund, and one real estate fund.

Let's assume an investor who is 35 years old, has been building her portfolio since she graduated college some 12 years earlier, and has already accumulated $200,000 in wealth. Given that she'll want to allocate 25% of her portfolio to bonds, her portfolio might be allocated as follows:

FUND	ALLOCATION
Bonds	$ 50,000
Stocks	$ 75,000
Real Estate	$ 75,000
Total	$ 200,000

For the sake of our example, let's pretend that no additional capital is invested in the portfolio, and rather than receiving cash distributions, all dividends are automatically reinvested back into the fund that that they are paid from. Therefore, dividends will basically function as capital gains. With time each fund will either increase in value or decrease in value. The chance that a fund will only move sideways is real but mainly applicable to our fixed income bond fund. While it would be fun to watch all of our investments appreciate, we have to accept that this will not always be the case, as short-term movements can go in either direction, and downturns can last anywhere from several months to upwards of a decade.

In this example, a year passes and our investor experiences a nice gain of 15% in her stock fund. The real estate market, however, did not perform well, and the fund decreases in value by 10.5%. She earned interest at a fixed rate of 2.25% on the bond fund, and with a fluctuation in value due to the fed funds rate increasing, the fund actually decreased in value by 2.5%, for an annualized loss of -0.25%. Therefore, the value of her portfolio changes as follows:

FUND	ALLOCATION	RETURN	NEW BALANCE	WEIGHT
Bonds	$ 50,000	-0.25%	49,875	24.54%
Stocks	$ 75,000	15.00%	86,250	42.44%
Real Estate	$ 75,000	-10.50%	67,125	33.03%
Total	$ 200,000		203,250	

On the plus side, she made money. $3,250 is not a huge annual return on a $200,000 portfolio, but the real estate market went into a correction and an increase to the fed funds rate took a small toll on her bond fund. As a long-term investor she should expect better average returns in the future. Yet there's no guarantee of what her returns will look like over the next several years. And though money was made, which is her primary objective, the bond and real estate markets both exhibited negative correlation with regard to the stock market, and as a result the portfolio is no longer in balance. Where 37.5% of the portfolio used to be allocated to both stocks and real estate, she now has 42.44% allocated to stocks and 33.03% allocated to real estate. The percent allocated to bonds has hardly changed, and if we round up just slightly we could say that it still rests at 25%. But our investor is now a year older and therefore one year closer to retirement. She wants a bit more safety, which means that she should now allocate 26% of her portfolio to bonds.

How is our investor going to get her asset allocation back on track? The only way to get there is to sell some of the stock fund and invest the proceeds in the bond and real estate funds. And for many investors this approach will seem counterintuitive. *She did well with her stock investment, so why on earth would she want to sell some of it to invest in the real estate market, especially after she lost 10.5% on this investment?*

The truth is, the stock market will not trend upward indefinitely. It will eventually encounter some sort of correction, *or even a crash.* By selling enough stocks to get her portfolio back in balance, our investor recognizes some of her gains. If stocks continue to go up the following year, and if they also outperform both the bond and real estate markets, then our investor will sell even more of her stock fund in order to reinvest in other markets. She's not trying to predict the top of the market and sell all of her stocks at once. Instead, she'll continue to rebalance her portfolio at least annually, and this will force her to progressively take more and more gains from her stock fund as the market approaches its top. When it finally falls, the rebalancing strategy will then force her to sell shares from whatever markets are performing well, and she'll reinvest the proceeds back into stocks after market conditions have forced the price lower.

After having rebalanced for the stock gains that she recognized upon turning 36, the pie will be a tad larger, and by increasing the bond allocation to 26%, it will also be a tad safer.

Our investor just bought more real estate at a discount. We know that she will continue to do this if stocks keep going up and real estate keeps going down. *But what happens when real estate starts to do well?* When the real estate market recovers and begins to outperform both stocks and bonds, then rebalancing will force her to sell some of her real estate shares in order to invest in both stocks and bonds. And if both stocks and real estate tank, then thank goodness she maintained her allocation to bonds, because the act of rebalancing will force her to sell a portion of her "safe" assets in order to invest in both of the equity markets after they've been beaten down and are selling at discount prices.

To continue our example, let's say that over the next year we get a stock correction, causing her fund to decline by 10.5%. Adding insult to injury, the performance of the real estate market is lackluster, and we see gains of only 4.5%, mainly because the fund continued to receive rents while property values moseyed along. Our bond fund, however, did its job. Interest payments came in at 2.5% while the fund rose in value by 0.75%, providing for a combined return of 3.25%. By the time our investor turns 37 her portfolio will be as follows:

FUND	ALLOCATION	RETURN	NEW BALANCE	WEIGHT
Bonds	52,845	3.25%	54,562	26.85%
Stocks	75,203	-10.50%	67,306	33.12%
Real Estate	75,203	4.50%	78,587	38.67%
Total	$ 203,250		200,455	

Again, the performance isn't impressive. In fact, our investor lost just about everything she made during the prior year. But it's important to note that the results could have been worse. Remember, at the end of the prior year she sold some of the stock fund to buy more of the real estate fund. If she hadn't rebalanced then the decline would have hit the portfolio harder. She'd have been more heavily invested in the stock fund, which lost value, and not as heavily invested in the real estate fund, which increased in value. During the first year the process of rebalancing forced her to chip away at some of her gains while reinvesting in the losing (or discounted) fund. There is indeed a benefit to rebalancing. And our investor does not need to predict market direction in order to recognize this benefit. She simply needs to continue with her rebalancing strategy, so long as she's invested in the right markets. Both stocks and real estate can be expected to beat inflation over the long-haul. And investing in the right mix of bonds will provide safety along with returns that also beat inflation. Over a prolonged investment span our investor can expect her average returns to exceed what is illustrated here. It all comes down to the fact that markets move in cycles. If our investor rebalances her portfolio as her different holdings progress through their cycles, she'll do much better than she would by simply buying each of her holdings and not touching them again until retirement. That's the power of rebalancing. And when used in conjunction with compounded dividends, the portfolio will be destined for success.

Market Cycles

In the above example we saw the impact of rebalancing over a short period of time, and for both years the results weren't exactly stellar. The net gain during the first year was small and the net loss during the second year wasn't too damaging. This can be the case over short intervals of a year or two, though it's possible for portfolios to experience large gains and losses over equally short periods of time. The entire point of combining asset classes that do not exhibit strong positive correlation is to minimize portfolio volatility. It's fine if individual markets exhibit volatility. This is where rebalancing provides an edge. But if the right markets are combined, then a bear market that is severe enough to drag down the entire portfolio will be minimized in terms of both depth and duration. Even during a recession, not all asset classes will perform poorly, and this helps contain the negative impact that affected markets have over the greater portfolio. When dividends are paid on each of the funds, it creates further insulation against market downturns. If a fund that yields 3% takes a 7% dip for the year, then damage done to the portfolio is contained at 4%, and further investments made during this period are purchased at a discount.

What we've learned about correlation tells us that we don't want our investments progressing through their market cycles in unison. *But what exactly is a market cycle, how long can we expect them to last, and how do they work to our advantage?* In short, a market completes a cycle as it moves from its top to a bottom and then back again. The stock market going into a bear market, recovering, and then setting a new high is a perfect example.

When the stock market has been beaten down a bottom will eventually form as a result of experienced investors recognizing that discounts are available. At some point they will begin buying in earnest as less-savvy investors continue to sell. This will at some point culminate in the amount of stocks being bought exceeding those that are being sold, and when this happens the market moves up from its bottom and continues in an upward direction. As it progresses higher, market sentiment improves, which in turn attracts more buyers into the market. It's never a straight line. But as the recovery progresses, media coverage will shift away from the negative forecasts they previously published to focus on projections that the worst is over. This in turn brings even more buyers back into the market. Eventually the majority will return and they will not only invest with funds that they withdrew as the market was going down, but also invest new funds that they earned from their work. This can continue for an extended period of time. Even as once underpriced stocks become overpriced, buyers will continue to throw money at the market. Media coverage now reports that markets are doing well. At this stage the experienced investors who purchased at the bottom begin to get out. While the rest of the market is caught up in a state of euphoria the smart money packs up their earnings and goes home. They will either hold their funds in cash or invest in a different market that they consider underpriced. The average investor, on the other hand, is left holding the bag. The market has peaked and as it begins to move downwards there will be speculation as to whether or not a new top has been set. Any move upward, however slight, will be viewed as an indicator that the market will regain its traction. But it doesn't. The good times are over. Different investors will accept this at different stages. And the market will proceed downward until we're finally back where we started. Most investors are scared. The media begins publishing report after report about how bleak the market conditions are. And experienced investors eventually get back in, buying up stocks at deep discounts.

It all sounds very organized and predictable. If experienced investors can get in and out as markets bottom and then peak, why can't we? The truth is that many investors try, but only a few succeed. And of those who achieve some success, the number that consistently succeeds is even smaller. There are all kinds of peaks and valleys as the market progresses through its cycle. And there is all kinds of speculation as to what constitutes a change in direction and what was nothing more than random noise. Is the market experiencing a 10 % correction or is there going to be a 30% drop? And those experienced investors who do buy in after a 30% drop, how much money do they have on the sidelines at times when markets are going higher and higher? What kind of gains and dividends do they miss out on? And where would they be right now had they rebalanced through the peaks and valleys instead of waiting for what they perceive to be the correct entry and exit points?

For the average investor, emotions play a role. If they can't afford to lose what they have invested then they are likely to cash out too early. Will they come to regret the decision and buy back in after markets have moved higher? How much damage can one investor inflict on their portfolio if they read the signals wrong? And for how much time can they remain idle if they sell too early or buy too soon? The entire premise of *Dividend Investing* is that we don't have to make these difficult and often emotionally driven decisions. What we are doing won't be nearly as profitable as putting everything on the line when the market bottoms and then taking it off when the market tops. It will, however, be much more achievable. And success won't just be achieved through the first market cycle, but will be repeated through every cycle we encounter over the course of our investing careers.

The benefit of investing in multiple markets is that they don't move through the cycles at the same time. What we're really concerned about are long-term movements. Are there periods when stocks and REITs move in opposite directions for extended periods of time? And how long does it take these cycles to reverse?

The key is to maintain your allocation to the selected asset classes for years, and allow them to pass through their various cycles. A secular stock market cycle will last on average 17 years, so the true benefits of asset allocation are likely to increase for investors holding their portfolio at least 20 years, and will become even more profound over 30 to 40 year periods. Just like the benefit of compounding dividends, the benefit of rebalancing through multiple market cycles is achieved only by the long-term investor. In the short-term the net impact of a rebalancing strategy could be a loss. Funds that you need back in less than five to ten years should not be invested in this manner.

Asset Class Subcategories

Because correlation is not static, I cannot provide numerical correlations between different asset classes. This is for the investor to research at the time they structure their portfolio. You'll want to start with asset classes that are not strongly correlated, such as stocks, bonds, and real estate, and then break your investments within each of these classes down further to capture different subclasses that also don't exhibit strong positive correlation. For stocks, we've discussed different market segments and seen that defensive stocks behave different from growth stocks. For REITs, there's a big difference between an equity REIT and a mortgage REIT. Within equity REITs, residential real estate could move through cycles in intervals that are different from those of commercial real estate. And economic factors that drag down corporate bonds might not have an impact on Treasuries. When we throw foreign markets into the mix, we again see that not all stocks, bonds, and real estate move through their cycles in tandem. In other words, not all stocks exhibit strong positive correlation. And the same applies to bonds and real estate. This is good. Because we can seek exposure within asset classes through funds that peak and dip in different intervals. This aids our endeavor to buy low and sell high through a systematic rebalancing approach.

Researching historical correlations can provide a hint at future correlations, but like anything in the investment world, it does not provide a guarantee. If enough (but not too many) funds are combined, it shouldn't matter if certain assets become strongly correlated at certain points in time. The impact will not be indefinite, and when a pair of funds does become strongly correlated for extended periods of time, it will be offset by movements in other asset classes and subclasses.

Adding subclasses to the portfolio is a great way to increase not only the benefits of diversification, but the corresponding benefits achieved through rebalancing. These benefits will decrease if you hold more than 10 or 12 funds. You want your asset classes and subclasses to work through their cycles independently. When too many funds are held it spreads your capital too thinly. When it comes time to rebalance, you'll be scooping less off the top of certain funds, as you add less to the bottom of others . On top of that, the commissions incurred while rebalancing will increase.

How Often Do You Need To Rebalance?

Now that we understand both the concept of rebalancing and the duration of time that it takes markets to work through their cycles, it's time to set our plan in motion. After we've determined what to invest in, and the proportion of the portfolio that we want to allocate to each of our asset classes and subclasses, we need to determine how often to rebalance the portfolio.

It's crucial that we not only determine our rebalancing schedule at the onset, but that we adhere to the plan after it's set in motion. If we deviate for the wrong reason it can have an adverse impact on the portfolio. It's okay to change the plan under certain circumstances. And these circumstances should be defined in advance. Perhaps you've increased the size of your monthly contribution and it now makes sense to rebalance more frequently. We'll see shortly that having larger holdings can make it beneficial to reallocate more often, especially if the commission is set at a fixed amount. But changing the frequency because stocks just went up and you want to grab your gains now is a bad idea. This type of decision is highly influenced by existing market conditions, which means the decision is essentially another form of market timing. We want to avoid this at all costs, because changing the rebalancing strategy along the way will open the door for transforming a very mechanical process into one that's influenced by emotions. We have nothing to gain by trying to adapt a rebalancing strategy to current market conditions. The entire point is that market conditions of all kinds aid the rebalancing strategy. If we follow through with our plan, then the market will bring the returns to us. It's that simple.

In the above example our investor rebalanced her portfolio annually. This is the minimum duration that you should wait before rebalancing the portfolio. If you wait longer then you're giving the markets too much time to reverse their movements, and this will rob you of the buy low, sell high opportunities that you're after. In addition, if you rebalance less frequently than once a year the portfolio will not maintain the desired allocation, and this could expose the portfolio to unnecessary risk.

It should also be noted that rebalancing doesn't have to be contingent on the passing of time. Some investors rebalance based on the size of a departure from their desired asset allocation. Say an investor is 54 years old, meaning that 44% of his portfolio is allocated to bonds. He might have decided long ago that he will rebalance the portfolio whenever it strays plus or minus 5% from the desired holding. So as markets move, he will rebalance only when bonds make up either 39% (or less) or 49% (or more) of the portfolio. Once rebalanced, no further rebalancing will be implemented until the allocation is again plus or minus 5% from the desired weight. There's an advantage to this approach. If you rebalance based on the size of a departure rather than a set interval of time, you increase the chances that you will buy and sell at or near market bottoms and tops, respectively. Over a period of 20 to 40 years this can have a profound impact on performance. The downside, of course, is that you can't just plug the next rebalancing date into your calendar and then go take a nap. You have to routinely monitor the portfolio in order to ensure that you rebalance at the appropriate time.

There's also an advantage to rebalancing semi-annually or quarterly. By increasing the frequency from annually to either of these two intervals, you again increase the chances that you will (*on occasion*) buy or sell at or near a market bottom or top. The downside is that you might rebalance at times when there hasn't been much of an opportunity for markets to move, and this will cause you to incur a commission with very little benefit. If commissions are low, this might be a moot point. But a dollar spent is a dollar spent, no matter how you slice it. The more frequently you rebalance, the greater the commissions you will incur, and doing so too frequently will erode the benefit.

The size of your portfolio could also be a driving factor when deciding how frequently to rebalance. We're not trading in and out of different asset classes. Rather, we're skimming off the top of our winners and using the proceeds to invest further in asset classes that have declined in value. When the portfolio is still young there might not be much to skim. In this case, it makes sense to only rebalance annually and then increase the frequency as your portfolio grows. The cost of rebalancing is, of course, an additional factor.

If you use a discount broker you'll incur a set fee for each trade, where a full service broker is likely to charge a commission structured as a percentage of the capital traded. I recommend the discount broker for investors who are self-directed and don't require handholding.

Say, for example, you can get $5.00 trades from your discount broker or a 0.5% commission from a full service broker. If investing $1,000 in a single fund it will cost $5.00 from either the discount broker or the full service broker. But if investing $10,000 you still only pay $5.00 with the discount broker, where the full service broker will charge you $50.00 (because 0.5% of $10,000 is $50). The point is not to pick between these two brokers (we would never want a full service broker who structures their fees this way, but they do exist and are unfortunately very prevalent in the financial world). Instead, we want to understand how the $5.00 commission from the discount broker functions as a static fee in terms of dollars, yet serves as a variable fee in terms of the percent paid. If investing $100 you will pay a 5% commission. If investing $1,000 you will pay a 0.5% commission. And if investing $10,000 you will pay a 0.005% commission. Yet it's consistently a $5 commission regardless of the order size. Where the full service broker will charge the same percent no matter the size of the trade, the discount broker is essentially offering greater discounts on larger trades—*hence, our preference for this service.*

This commission structure doesn't just apply to new investments, but to trades executed in order to rebalance the portfolio. When you first start out the amount of capital moved each time you rebalance will be quite small. As your portfolio grows, you'll see that the amounts moved increase in size, meaning that your commission expressed as a percentage keeps getting smaller. The goal is for each commission paid to be as small a percent of the trade as possible. It doesn't matter that it's only $5. We want to think in terms of percentages. We know from above what an extra 1% will compound to over a 40 year investment horizon. So you're better off rebalancing every quarter if it only costs 1% per quarter, but if it's going to cost 4% then you might want to wait and rebalance annually. Statistically speaking, taking steps to ensure that the fee is a small percent of the capital being moved will compound to your advantage.

Early on it makes sense to rebalance annually, as this keeps commissions low. But once you're at the point where you could rebalance semi-annually or even quarterly for less than 1%, go ahead and do so. At that point catching market movements will outweigh the expense of incurring more frequent commissions. But when the portfolio is small and commissions are upwards of 4% per trade, it's possible that markets will need to move by as much as 8% in order for rebalancing to be beneficial. Remember, you incur the commission not just when you sell shares, but again when you reinvest the proceeds.

Here's an example. Say you're just starting out and you have $7,500 invested with 1/3 in bonds and 2/3 in stocks. By the end of the first quarter your stock fund is up 4% and your bond fund is down 4%. Given that more is invested in stocks than in bonds, your portfolio has a net gain of 1.33% (100 / 7,500 = 0.0133). So in order to rebalance based on this $100 net gain, you will need to sell $133.33 worth of the stock fund in order to buy $133.33 worth of the bond fund. Does it make sense to rebalance in this situation?

	Beginning Allocation	Change in Value	New Allocation	Desired Allocation
Bonds	2,500	(100)	2,400	2,533.33
Stocks	5,000	200	5,200	5,066.67
Total	7,500	100	7,600	7,600

The answer is a resounding "*No*". You will pay a $5 commission on each trade (once to sell your stock fund, and again to buy the bond fund). This will cost $10. In order for rebalancing quarterly to be worthwhile, the bond fund will need to outperform the stock fund by 7.5% over the next quarter. The $10 total commission equates to 7.5% of the amount being moved (10 / 133.33 = 0.075). So bonds will need to perform well comparatively in order for the $10 commission to be recouped. At such an early stage in your investing career it's best to keep expenses (expressed as a percentage of your trades) low. Therefore, an annual rebalancing schedule should be implemented.

Down the road that $5.00 commission per trade will start to feel like small potatoes. And at that point rebalancing more frequently, up to four times per year, will start to make sense. Once you have a total of $75,000 invested, a 4% dip in bonds combined with a 4% gain in stocks will require you to reallocate $1,333.33 from the stock fund to the bond fund.

	Beginning Allocation	Change in Value	New Allocation	Desired Allocation
Bonds	25,000	(1,000)	24,000	25,333.33
Stocks	50,000	2,000	52,000	50,666.67
Total	75,000	1,000	76,000	76,000

A total commission of $10 on these trades equates to 0.75% of the total capital being moved. At this point it isn't even worth contemplating whether or not a 0.75% commission is a necessary expense. Go ahead and rebalance on the schedule that is right for you—*be it quarterly or biannually*—and don't ever stray from this schedule simply because you think a certain market might be at its top, or a different market might be at its bottom. We're not trying to time the market. Instead, we're implementing a systematic approach that will make our gains exceed our losses, and we eliminate the likeliness of human error as we do so.

How to Keep Commissions Even Lower: *Dollar Cost Averaging As You Rebalance*

Those who are both fee-conscious and forward-thinking may have already pieced together that you incur a commission not just when you rebalance, but also as you dollar cost average. *So why not rebalance and buy new shares at the same time? It makes sense, doesn't it?*

An investor who is young in his career and working an entry level position likely won't be contributing as much as an older investor who has stayed with the same company and worked her way into a higher paying job. It pays to start investing young no matter the size of your contribution. But from a fee perspective, if your goal is to save $200 per month it doesn't make sense to split that amount between a stock fund and a real estate fund and then buy into each of them every month. You'll pay at least a $5.00 commission on each trade, meaning that your portfolio needs to earn a 5% return before you break even. It would make more sense to buy in quarterly, but alternate funds each quarter, with $600 going entirely to stocks the first quarter, $600 entirely to real estate the second quarter, and so forth. In this scenario if commissions are still $5.00 then you're paying less than 1% per trade. With time your dividend income will increase, and if you reinvest it along with your quarterly contributions, then the commission will get smaller and smaller each month.

At the beginning rebalancing might not even be an option. When your portfolio is young, even a 10% movement might equate to selling just one or two shares of your winning fund in order to buy one or two shares of your losing fund. At this stage you're better off to forgo rebalancing and save on commissions. If you're really young with the dedication to scrape up whatever extra cash you can just to hurl at the market, it's not even necessary to diversify outside of domestic stocks. In your early twenties if you want to just keep commissions low and put everything in an index fund that tracks the S&P 500 (SPY), you'll be fine. And don't worry about whether it goes up or down in the short-term. If your returns aren't gigantic 45 years from now, it will be the first time in history that something like that has ever happened. Even if you do run into a bear market early on (which again is good, so long as you don't panic and sell), then just keep at it and buy up whatever you can. You'll be handsomely rewarded with a recovery, and this will put you in a good position to diversify and begin your rebalancing regimen.

The two-fund example discussed above is presented purely to illustrate a point. It shows the impact of commissions over the benefit of rebalancing. In practice, you might have your investments spread out amongst 10 different funds, and given that most discount brokers charge between $5.00 and $8.00 per trade, it could cost anywhere from $50 to $80 when you dollar cost average into these funds. If your monthly contribution is small, wait until the end of the quarter to make the actual investment. This will keep commissions, when viewed as a percentage of your invested capital, low. But if you start earning a higher salary and contributing enough each month that your commissions as a percent of your contribution is now less than 1%, go ahead and invest it monthly. The same logic we applied to rebalancing can be applied here. The only difference is that we can kill two birds with one stone. Yes, it's a little extra math, but we should rebalance the portfolio as we make new investments. There's no point in incurring a separate set of commissions to rebalance.

Let's look at an example. Our investor has built a well-diversified portfolio worth $170,000. He's 35 years old and therefore has allocated 25% of the portfolio to bonds. Most of this goes to Treasuries because he wants to keep the funds safe, but corporate bonds are also included, as the added yield gives the allocation a nice boost over inflation. His REIT holdings are also well-diversified, with the majority allocated to equity REITs and small allocations to both mortgage REITs and foreign REITs. His stock allocation is more heavily weighted towards growth, while also including a healthy allocation to blue chips, and some added exposure to both preferred and foreign stocks. All of the holdings will pay a dividend of some sort, and while our investor wants to take advantage of compounding returns, at his age he also wants the impact that growth has on a portfolio.

Over the course of the next quarter capital gains and losses are incurred, and his funds change in value as shown below, providing a net return of $3,283. This is a nice return, especially when you consider that 25% of the portfolio is invested in bonds. That, and his dividend income is not yet factored into the equation. Annualized, it equates to a gain of 7.73% (or about 1.93% for the quarter).

	Beginning Allocation	Change in Value	New Allocation	Desired Allocation	Buy / (Sell)
Treasurie Bonds - 15%	25,500	159	25,659	25,992	333
Corporate Bonds - 7.5%	12,750	74	12,824	12,996	172
Junk Bonds -2.5%	4,250	-21	4,229	4,332	103
Mortgage REIT - 2.5%	4,250	175	4,425	4,332	-93
Equity REIT - 12.5%	21,250	638	21,888	21,660	-228
Foreign REIT - 7.5%	12,750	-117	12,633	12,996	363
Blue Chip Stocks - 15%	25,500	829	26,329	25,992	-337
Growth Stocks - 20%	34,000	1,275	35,275	34,657	-618
Preferred Stocks - 10%	17,000	-64	16,936	17,328	392
Foreign Stocks - 7.5%	12,750	335	13,085	12,996	-89
Total	170,000	3,283	173,283	173,283	-

Is it worth the cost of commission for our investor to rebalance? If his discount broker charges $8 per trade and he has 10 funds, then it will cost him $80 to rebalance. This equates to a charge of 2.44% for the capital being moved (80 / 3,283 = 0.0244). This is above our 1% rule, and it means that the fund will need to earn net returns of at least 2.44% per quarter in order for there to be a benefit, or an annualized return of 9.75%. Remember, it won't just cost our investor $80 to rebalance this quarter, but will cost him $80 each quarter that he rebalances. So the benefit of rebalancing needs to recur each quarter, otherwise it's better to rebalance annually.

Under strong economic conditions many portfolios will indeed generate average returns in the neighborhood of 9.75%, but with 25% of the portfolio allocated to bonds, consistently earning returns at or above this level will be a stretch. Granted, some years he might do really well and earn more than 9.75%, but there will be times when his equities will decline and the total portfolio return won't even match the interest paid on bonds. In fact, some years it might go negative. On average, 9.75% per year is ambitious, and the decision to incur rebalancing fees should not be based on where our investor thinks the market will go next.

If our investor is also dollar cost averaging as he rebalances, then he will have additional capital to invest. And these two actions combined could bring the commission paid down below 1%. It all depends on how much he contributes. If he's able to contribute $1,000 per month and wants to rebalance quarterly, then the total amount being moved around is now $6,283. If he incurs $80 in commissions, then this brings the cost down to 1.27%. If he decides instead to rebalance every four months, then it will cost him 1.10%. We're splitting hairs at this point. And many investors would probably proceed with their dollar cost averaging/rebalance strategy. When we consider the impact of dividends, this approach definitely makes sense. Because we aren't just able to dollar cost average and rebalance in one shot, but can actually dollar cost average, rebalance, and reinvest our dividends all at the same time. And if we assume that a reasonable amount of dividend income was earned on the holdings, the amount of money being moved around goes up, and the cost of the commission goes down.

With dividend income we get an extra $1,798 (in practice it might not be this exact amount, and will likely change each quarter, but this provides a reasonable approximation for our example). Even though the total to buy/(sell) only amounts to $4,798 ($3,000 in new contributions and $1,798 in dividend income), we're really moving around $8,081. The gains and losses that we're rebalancing with should be viewed in terms of absolute dollars. Like in our previous example, when we move $133.33 from stocks to bonds, we should think of it as moving the full $133.33. This doesn't create new capital for the portfolio. We now have more shares of the bond fund and fewer shares of the stock fund. So the immediate impact on the portfolio nets to zero. But for the sake of determining when to rebalance, we should treat this as a positive $133.33. In the current example, our investor is rebalancing $3,283 in gains/losses that sum to zero. When he throws in $3,000 in new capital and $1,799 in reinvested dividends, the total comes to $8,082.

3,000 + 1,799 = 4,799

4,799 + 3,283 = 8,082

	New Contribution	Dividend Income	Rebalance	Buy / (Sell)
Treasurie Bonds - 15%	450	239	333	1,022
Corporate Bonds - 7.5%	225	90	172	487
Junk Bonds -2.5%	75	96	103	274
Mortgage REIT - 2.5%	75	239	-93	221
Equity REIT - 12.5%	375	359	-228	506
Foreign REIT - 7.5%	225	138	363	726
Blue Chip Stocks - 15%	450	175	-337	288
Growth Stocks - 20%	600	128	-618	110
Preferred Stocks - 10%	300	215	392	907
Foreign Stocks - 7.5%	225	120	-89	256
Total	3,000	1,799	-	4,799

So what does $80 over $8,082 come to? It's just a smidgen under 1%. And this is much better than paying 2.44%, which over the course of a year would be 9.75%. *Ouch! That would really hurt the portfolio!* At 1% per quarter it only costs 4% per year to rebalance. And I bet you already know what I'm going to say about the annualized savings of 5.75%—*yes, compound it over the remaining 30 years that our investor has until retirement!* As time goes on and the portfolio gets bigger, the cost of the commission will work its way further and further below 1%. It just keeps getting smaller. These small amounts really do add up over time, which is why we really want to strive to implement a low-cost approach.

Impact of Rebalancing On Your Dividend Yield

It's important not to let dividend yield influence your asset allocation strategy. It might be tempting to do so because, after all, our goal is to accumulate as much dividend income as possible. We do want strong dividends, but proper asset allocation needs to come first. We want to control for risk. And while the markets we invest in do pay dividends, we do not want to override our tolerance for risk in an effort to increase dividend yield. If we control for risk and regularly rebalance, then as our investments move through their cycles, the size of the portfolio will increase. This will put more money into each of the asset classes we're invested in, including those that pay higher dividends.

We still care about dividend yield and the compounding effect it has on the portfolio. But after the asset classes have been allocated, the practice of rebalancing can change the total yield on the portfolio. There will be times when rebalancing forces us to sell a high yielding fund that has performed well in order to reinvest in a lower yielding fund that has underperformed. At other times just the opposite will happen. Selling a lower yielding fund in order to reinvest in a higher yielding fund will likewise increase the total dividend yield. But we can't force it. We have to let markets work through their cycles and make our trades systematically based on a rebalancing strategy.

It's the practice of holding a growth fund early in the investment horizon which in turn increases the pie, albeit slow and steady. We invest in the growth fund because we expect it to, on average, produce larger capital gains than our dividend payers. And as the growth fund outperforms, the practice of rebalancing will force us to progressively take gains from the growth fund and reinvest them in other higher yielding funds.

The game changes once we reach retirement. We still want to rebalance the portfolio. In fact, we'll do this for the rest of our lives in order to control for risk. But market cycles can cause the buying and selling to persist in a certain direction for years, and this can progressively decrease (and at other times increase) our dividend distributions.

There are going to be times when it isn't practical for the retired investor to stick to their rebalancing plan. At this stage we're more concerned about generating enough income to live off of than we are with capital appreciation. Regardless of how diligently you built your portfolio and structured your plan, be prepared to deviate from your strategy. When interest rates are cut to near-zero, there will be cause for concern and action should be taken. Treasuries may be perceived as safe, but the interest rate risk that all bondholders face is very real. Even if your bond funds continue to beat inflation, when inflation stagnates your interest payments might not provide enough income to meet your spending needs. A low-interest-rate environment can force bondholders to seek other forms of income, particularly in retirement.

Reducing the fed funds rate to near-zero is a strategic tactic used to stimulate a poor economy. When interest rates are low people are more likely to buy a house or a car, and businesses are more likely to borrow funds in order to pursue new projects. This can make life difficult for the 75 year-old retiree who has 65% of her portfolio allocated to bonds. The capital is safe, but the interest payments become lackluster. And the long-term benefit of allowing markets to work through their prolonged cycles is no longer relevant. I have two recommendations for dealing with this type of situation, and it's to our retired investor's advantage to implement both of them.

First, all retired investors should have a cash reserve to spend from should their passive income distributions fall below the desired level. Just like the working investor who wants to keep at least six month's worth of salary on reserve in the event of a job loss, our retired investor should also maintain a cash reserve. It should be held outside of the portfolio in either a money market account or in CDs (whichever will provide a higher level of interest). But for the retired investor, a six month reserve is much too small. A reserve along the lines of five year's worth of living expenses is more desirable. This gives our investor something to spend from should her living expenses begin to exceed her dividend income. If instead of spending from her reserve, our investor liquidates a portion of her bond funds, it will permanently reduce the income she earns for the rest of her life. Dividends are paid per share, and if we reduce the number of shares in order to spend, the impact will be permanent.

If you're asking yourself how to build a reserve equal to five year's worth of living expenses, then you're starting to think like a responsible investor. Yes, this is an ambitious goal. It requires effort and discipline to get there. Maybe even a little luck, because we all know that life can throw us curve balls. Even before you near retirement, you should already have six month's worth of salary on reserve. So you'll need to pinch the rest of the reserve from someplace, and that's not always easy. But remember, as you're approaching retirement your dividend income should be stacking up. You'll be in the process of shifting from growth funds to strong dividend payers. Assuming you're on track to retirement, you may want to take a pause from reinvesting your dividends and use them to build your reserve. The cash will earn interest, so the benefit of compounding will persist even though your dividends have been temporarily diverted to a different objective. And the best part about this approach is that it allows you to build a reserve without selling any shares. If you can't get all the way there before retirement, this might provide incentive to live below your means in the early years, and then gradually increase your lifestyle as the reserve comes together.

Again, you'll want to earn as much interest as possible on the reserve without assuming any risk, including the risk inherent with even the safest of bonds. It's recommended that at least one year of the reserve be kept in a money market account so that the funds can be accessed without incurring a penalty. But if a higher interest rate can be earned on CDs, this is where the remainder of the funds should be kept. This can be done in a tiered approach. You'll want to hold CDs that mature in two, three, four, and five year increments. If you don't need the liquidity when a CD matures, go ahead and reinvest the funds for an appropriate length of time.

The second recommendation is to keep a large portion of your portfolio invested in long-term bond funds. A distinct advantage of investing in long-term bonds is that they have less income risk. While the value of the fund will fluctuate as interest rates change, the long-term fund will pay an interest rate premium, and the interest offered before rates are cut will be locked in for a longer duration. The distributions from these funds won't taper off as soon as interest rates decline. Instead, it's a lengthy process that occurs as the holdings within the fund are sold or mature and are then replaced with new long-term bonds purchased at the lower rate. While the price of a long-term bond fund will fluctuate more than the price of a short-term bond fund, the income from the long-term bond fund can be viewed as relatively stable and slow to change.

As we know, a small increase in the fed funds rate will cause the price of a long-term bond fund to fall more than the price of a short-term bond fund. But when the fed funds rate is cut, the price of a long-term bond fund will increase by more than the price of a short-term bond fund. In retirement, a healthy portion of the bond allocation should be allocated to a long-term Treasury fund, and here's why:

1) Interest rates on long-term bonds are generally higher than on short-term bonds, so the investor is rewarded for holding a long-term bond fund.

2) When interest rates rise it will have an adverse impact on the price of the fund. Our goal is not to live off of the price of the fund, it's to live off of distributions from the fund. So there is no reason to sell at this point in the market cycle.

3) When interest rates fall the price of the bond fund will increase, and given that the fund is holding long-term bonds, it takes time for the fund holdings to mature and be replaced with the new, lower-yielding bonds. This means that when poor economic conditions dictate that the fed funds rate be cut to near-zero for a prolonged period of time, we not only have a profit opportunity should we sell the fund, but the nature of a long-term fund means that we have plenty of time to react to the change. The decision to sell doesn't have to be made overnight, and we can sell the fund in shifts over the course of several years, all the while reinvesting in other instruments that deliver the return we require, like stocks and real estate.

In other words, a long-term bond fund provides the retired investor with an opportunity to earn a higher rate of interest than is available through a short-term fund. When interest rates are cut, or even slashed, it puts upward pressure on the price of the fund, and this creates a selling opportunity. This selling opportunity allows the retired investor to buy up higher-yielding equities. While we might not want to sell our entire holding in the long-term fund, we can sell more than our rebalancing strategy otherwise calls for in order to secure adequate dividend income. It won't be necessary to reduce our capital; we'll simply divert that capital to a stronger yielding market.

Yes, this approach does teeter on the edge of a market timing strategy. But the goal here is preservation, in terms of both invested capital and dividend distribution. We're not trying to time entry and exit points, but simply making an effort to preserve what we've built. With any strategy that incorporates a bit of market timing, there is room for human error and also no guarantee that the markets won't move against you. In retirement, a pure rebalancing strategy eliminates that risk of human error but leaves the portfolio exposed to interest rate risk, especially after you've allocated more than half of your portfolio to bonds. I don't recommend implementing this strategy without first accumulating a five-year cash reserve. It will provide a cushion and reduce the need to reallocate the entire bond holding.

It's always best to implement a strategy that doesn't require you to change course based on market direction. This scenario, of course, is a true exception because we can neither control for interest rate risk nor continue to collect adequate interest income when rates are slashed.

Chapter 13

Tax Implications

I've saved the best for last! And yes, that was sarcasm. Let's face it, nobody likes taxes. And after we're done paying them, we don't really care to read about them. It's because there's no excitement in taxes, no opportunities to create wealth. It's not a game that you gain from, like investing, but rather a game where you're forced to protect what's already yours. And you're required to play whether you like it or not.

Yes, we have to pay taxes. But we're allowed to structure our holdings in a manner that reduces our tax liability to the furthest extent permitted by the tax code. There are huge benefits to understanding how taxes work, not just for the dividend investor, but for all investors. We're going to take a look at how dividends are taxed, and we're also going to have a look at how each of our asset classes is taxed. The goal isn't to become a tax expert, but to gain a basic understanding of how each of our investments is taxed. We won't avoid a solid investment strategy because of the tax implications. *Dividend Investing* advocates a long-term investment strategy based on dollar cost averaging, asset allocation, and rebalancing, with reinvested dividends serving as the catalyst that both boosts returns and provides income in retirement. We can't sacrifice the art of our execution because the tax man might come knocking. We have to let him knock. And whatever we owe him, then that's what we'll pay.

It's important to control for risk, even if most interest payments are generally taxed heavier than most stock dividends. But if you're juggling multiple accounts with different tax implications, then understanding taxes can help ensure that each index fund is held in the account that benefits you the most.

For those of you investing solely in a tax-deferred account, such as an IRA or a 401(k), the implications are simple. Everything in the account will be taxed as ordinary income upon withdrawal, regardless of what you're invested in. Your strategy should be based on the asset mix that is right for you given your tolerance for risk. The same applies to a non-taxable account, such as a Roth IRA. Here, your contribution is made with after-tax dollars, and your withdrawals are tax-free. It doesn't matter what instruments you use to build wealth inside the account, or how the returns would have been taxed if they were held outside the account. When you make a withdrawal there aren't any taxes, so your investment strategy should again be based solely on the asset mix that is right for you given your tolerance for risk.

It gets trickier when investments are held in a regular taxable account, and even more so if you're juggling investments between both a taxable and a tax-deferred or non-taxable account. The approach I advocate puts proper asset allocation and risk tolerance at the forefront, and the tax implications are a secondary concern. But if we maintain multiple accounts, then tax implications should be taken into consideration when deciding where to hold each of our investments. The heavier taxed assets should go into a tax-deferred account, while an investment that receives preferential tax treatment should be held in a fully taxable account. It sounds easy, but tax planning can be a tough job. We'll only be investing in three distinct asset classes, yet the tax implications are extensive.

From a compounding perspective, all distributions function as a dividend. But from a tax perspective, not all distributions are created equal. Even though tax implications are not the driving factor to our approach, you should never enter into an investment without understanding how it will be taxed.

Bonds form the basis of our risk control, yet interest income (on most bonds) is taxed heavier than dividend income (on most stocks). It might be tempting to overweight the portfolio in favor of a stock fund that receives preferential tax treatment. But remember, you want to own your age minus ten years in bonds, so once you turn 61 greater than half the portfolio should be invested in bond funds. And it's important not to deviate from this approach. The amount saved on taxes is incremental in comparison to the damage that stocks will endure during a bear market. So while there might be certain funds that we prefer over others in terms of tax treatment, it truly is a secondary consideration.

Tax Implications for ETFs

When holding an ETF, taxes are distributed based on the underlying assets. So if you buy an ETF that holds stocks, the distributions will be taxed as dividend income. If you buy an ETF that holds REITs, the distributions will be taxed as rent. And if you buy an ETF that holds bonds, the distributions will be taxed as interest.

It sounds simple, but the tax implications can be cumbersome. It all depends on the type of ETF held. If you buy a single ETF that holds stocks, bonds, and real estate, and perhaps even some foreign holdings from all three markets, the tax liability will be based on which of the assets in the fund generated the distribution. You might only receive one quarterly payment from the fund, but the portion of the distribution that came from the fund's REIT holdings will be treated as a rental payment, while the portion that came from the fund's bond holdings will be treated as an interest payment. In practice, we want to hold separate funds for each asset class because it aids in our rebalancing strategy, but for the sake of illustration, it's important to understand that ETFs are taxed differently depending on the assets held.

Regardless of how the investment is made (through an ETF, mutual fund, or direct purchase), there are two common tax triggers. Taxes are paid when you receive a dividend, rental payment, or interest payment. And taxes are paid on capital gains. If the asset is purchased directly, the tax is paid after the asset is sold for a gain. But if the asset is held in a fund, taxes are only due on the gain if it's distributed to the fundholder. The fundholder will receive the distribution just as they receive a dividend, but it will be treated as a capital gain for tax purposes.

There's a third trigger that's encountered when the investment is acquired through an ETF (or mutual fund). In addition to taxes being incurred as a result of the ETF distributing a gain, a tax is also encountered when the investor sells the ETF for a gain. This might sound like double counting, but it's not. In fact, the third trigger actually works to the investor's advantage. It doesn't result in more taxes, but rather serves as an opportunity for the investor to postpone taxes. Let's take a closer look at each of these triggers.

First, there's a tax on the dividend distribution. Depending on the ETF, the investor could receive stock dividends, rental payments, or interest. We'll see shortly that stock dividends are unique in that (1) they're subject to double taxation, and (2) the shareholder receives preferential treatment because of this double taxation. Interest and rents, on the other hand, are going to be taxed at the ordinary income tax rate, unless there's a provision that prevents them from being taxed at all.

The second trigger is the capital gains distribution. When the fund sells a holding, they pass the capital gain along to the fundholder in the same manner that they pass along a dividend. Again, taxes will be levied during the year that the capital gain is received. This puts the investor at a disadvantage in terms of tax planning. They have no control over when the fund will sell its holdings, and therefore can't defer the gain into subsequent years by maintaining the holding. This is where a passively managed ETF is truly superior to an actively managed mutual fund. With the ETF that holds an index, the buying and selling of securities within the fund is contingent on whether or not the index changes its constituents, and this means that capital gains are quite rare in comparison to that of an actively managed mutual fund. For example, the Dow Jones Industrial average has only changed constituents 52 times since its inception in 1896. With a bond index fund, it's possible to see more buying and selling as a means of controlling for the duration of bonds held. But the gains on a bond are generally much smaller than on a stock, so the tax consequences won't be too severe. The distributions from a REIT fund are a bit trickier, but there's a huge advantage here. If the REIT is still in the distribution phase of the lifecycle, meaning that the properties under management have not yet been fully depreciated, then the capital gains distribution is considered a return of capital and is not subject to tax. If you feel like you need your CPA to explain this to you, it's understandable. We'll dive deeper into this advantage when we focus solely on the taxation of REITs. By the time you're finished with the chapter you should have a good understand of how this works.

The third trigger occurs when the ETF is sold. For tax purposes, the investor will recognize either a gain or a loss depending on whether they made or lost money on the investment. Given our rebalancing strategy, you're much more likely to recognize gains than losses. This is good for building your portfolio, but it comes with a tax consequence. And it might feel like you're getting taxed twice, given that you're already paying taxes as the capital gains are distributed, but you're not. When a fund sells a holding at a gain you'll receive that gain in the form of a dividend, and you will pay taxes on it. But the distribution also reduces what's being held within the fund. The value of the fund goes up as the assets being held appreciate, and then goes back down when they sell an asset and distribute the gain. So what you're really taxed on when you sell an ETF is the gains that the fund has realized on the holdings that they haven't sold yet. And when it comes to an index fund, most of the holdings are simply held, and there's very little selling. This is particularly true of stock index funds. And it gives the investor a huge advantage, being that they can defer taxes by simply remaining invested in the fund.

Stocks

When it comes to stocks dividends, we pay taxes twice. There's no way around it. Companies pay their dividends out of after-tax earnings. This means that the company earned a profit, they paid taxes on that profit, and with the money that remains after paying taxes they pay a dividend to their shareholders. Once the shareholder receives the dividend they are taxed on the distribution, which means the same money has been taxed twice. Given that a share of stock represents an ownership interest in the company, we can't even think of it as two separate entities being taxed on their transactions. As a shareholder you are in fact an owner of the company (even if your ownership interest is incredibly small, it's still an ownership interest). And when the company pays taxes it reduces cash on the balance sheet, which means that the value of your investment is reduced in proportion to your share of the taxes paid. When you receive your dividend distribution you again pay taxes, though this time you will pay them directly rather than your investment decreasing in value by the amount of taxes due. This is why *certain* dividends receive preferential tax treatment. And the word *certain* is extremely important. In order for a dividend to receive preferential tax treatment it must be qualified. The rate might differ depending on your tax bracket, but generally, the tax charged on a qualified dividend is only 15%, where an ordinary dividend is taxed as ordinary income.

Regardless of the type of dividends paid, our goal is to gain broad exposure to the stock market. And depending on our tolerance for risk and our approach to diversification, we might also want some exposure to foreign markets. So before we purchase a fund, we'll want to understand how the dividends are taxed. The IRS states that "qualified dividends are dividends paid during the tax year from domestic corporations and qualified foreign corporations." This means that dividends paid out to shareholders of for-profit companies on either the New York Stock Exchange or the NASDAQ are generally recognized as qualified dividends and thus receive a reduced tax rate of 15%. A qualified foreign corporation would be a corporation whose stock is traded through American Depository Receipts (ADRs) or on a U.S. market. And dividends from these companies are also taxed at 15%. But there are still plenty of foreign companies out there whose dividends are taxed as an ordinary dividend. And we'll see in just a minute that even if the company qualifies for preferential treatment, the stock still needs to be held for a specified length of time in order for the dividend to remain qualified.

When you purchase a fund that invests in a variety of assets, it's possible that some of the distribution will be taxed as qualified dividends and some of the distribution will be taxed as ordinary dividends. This is another reason why we recommend investing in an index fund ETF over an actively managed mutual fund. It's easier to determine what an index fund is holding, which allows you to determine how the investment will be taxed.

If the index fund is holding nothing but domestic U.S. equities, it's a relatively safe bet that the entire dividend distribution will be taxed as a qualified dividend. When it comes to foreign equities it's not always black and white, and it's possible that the tax treatment won't be consistent for the entire distribution. Pulling the prospectus, or even sending an email to the fund, can help you determine the tax implications. If you work with a financial advisor, they should have information on how the investment will be taxed. But keep in mind, a financial advisor is different than a tax professional. While they should be able to inform you of the tax implications of your investments, they most likely will not provide tax planning strategies. If you're in a higher income tax bracket, you'll want to work with a tax accountant on this. Your financial advisor will teach you to implement a solid investment strategy first, and then acknowledge the tax implications that follow.

There are many types of distributions that don't qualify for preferential tax treatment. We'll discuss them in greater detail in our sections on bonds and REITs, but it's safe to conclude that distributions from the following vehicles will be taxed as ordinary income: REITs, MLPs (master limited partnerships), special one-time dividends, dividends paid on employee stock options, dividends paid on tax-exempt companies, and dividends paid on money market accounts.

There's one more catch that applies regardless of these qualifications. Assuming that you are holding common shares, you have to hold the stock for 61 days in order for the dividend to be qualified. And if you're holding preferred shares, you have to hold the stock for 91 days. Otherwise it will be taxed as an ordinary dividend regardless of the corporation's domesticity or qualifications.

Capital gains also receive preferential tax treatment, so long as the stock is held for at least one year. Just like qualified dividends, long-term capital gains (held for greater than one year) will be taxed at 15%, where short-term capital gains (held for less than one year) are taxed as ordinary income. The taxes, of course, are only paid on the amount by which the stock appreciated after buying it, not on the entire sales proceeds.

As investors, we don't like to incur losses, but from a tax perspective losses are good; they allow you to reduce your taxable gains, and then a portion of your earned income. Our rebalancing strategy increases the probability that we will incur gains rather than losses, but for the investor that chooses to allocate 5% of her portfolio to individual stock selections, it's very possible that she'll incur some losses along the way. It's best to hold individual stock picks in a fully taxable account, especially if the dividends are qualified. Yes, you'll have to pay tax on the dividends as they're received, rather than waiting until the funds are withdrawn, but you'll pay the tax at 15% rather than your regular tax rate. You're far more likely to incur a loss on an individual holding. With the indexes we'll be investing in, there should always be confidence that the index will come back. But an individual holding might take a hit and never recover. That, or you take a loss simply because you found a more attractive stock to invest in.

Losses are completely worthless inside of a retirement account. Instead of claiming a deduction, the loss simply lowers your account balance. You might view this as a tax savings down the road when you're required to make withdrawals, but that's only because you have fewer funds to withdraw and therefore fewer taxes to pay. This isn't the kind of tax savings we're after. The greater the likelihood that a loss will be incurred on an investment, the stronger the argument for holding the investment in a fully taxable account. This is the approach that should be applied when it comes to individual stocks.

So long as the loss is incurred in a taxable account, the IRS permits you to offset the loss against your gains. In the event that your loss exceeds your gains, the IRS permits you to offset a maximum of $3,000 against ordinary income, with the rest being carried forward and applied to subsequent gains (or another $3,000 in ordinary income for each year that the losses are carried forward). And we shouldn't have trouble coming up with gains. Our strategy forces us to automatically sell winners. Although we don't want to treat our individual selections as a stomping ground for tax deductions, when we do incur a loss we shouldn't be bashful about selling the stock and taking the tax deduction. The opportunities to recognize a loss as we rebalance will be fewer, though during economic pullbacks, it's possible for all of our markets to decline simultaneously, and we should anticipate that rebalancing will force us to recognize losses at certain points in our investing career. It's not a bad thing. When it comes to taxes there is no stigma with recognizing losses. They're actually assets rather than liabilities. And we already know that there are rewards to be reaped by allowing our holdings to pass through their cycles. If your rebalancing strategy dictates that you take a loss in a very organized and systematic fashion, then go ahead and recognize the loss. You'll pay fewer taxes because of it.

There is one additional caveat when it comes to losses—*the wash sale*. You don't get to recognize the tax benefit on a loss if you buy the asset back within 30 days. In other words, you can't sell one of your losers, reap the tax benefit, and then immediately buy the asset back. You need to wait at least 30 days, or invest the proceeds in an asset that is not the same or substantially identical. This applies to both funds and individual holdings. If you're invested in a fund that tracks the S&P 500, you can't sell it for a loss and then immediately invest in a different fund that tracks the S&P 500. The loss will be disallowed. Although the definition of "substantially identical" is not clearly defined by the IRS, your broker can report a wash sale to them on form 1099-B.

As far as dividend income is concerned, there is an advantage to holding your growth funds in a tax-deferred account. As you approach retirement, you might want to sell more of your low-yielding growth fund than your rebalancing strategy calls for, as this will permit you to reinvest in an income-generating fund. If you incur a big gain in a taxable account, you get a big tax bill, plain and simple. But in a tax-deferred account you can switch entirely from one fund to another without incurring the capital gains tax. This makes your retirement account an ideal place to hold your growth fund. The dividend income is low, so the benefit of paying the preferred rate of 15% in a fully taxable account is relatively small. When it's time to focus more on dividend income, you might want to switch entirely into REITs or the Dividend Aristocrats. And the ability to do so without a tax implication will protect your capital, and consequently allow for a bigger stream of dividend income.

Bonds

The tax complexities increase when we start adding bonds to the portfolio. The only common point of reference between our stock holdings and our bond holdings is the treatment of capital gains. If a bond is held for greater than one year before it's sold, we receive preferential treatment of 15% on the capital gain. Otherwise, it's taxed as ordinary income. The same applies to the gains recognized when we sell a bond fund. The taxation of bond interest, on the other hand, varies greatly between issues. The preferential treatment that we receive on our stock dividends won't apply to distributions from a bond fund, though in some cases the fundholder will be exempt from taxes at either the federal level or the state and local levels. It all depends on the type of bond and the residence of the holder. While the scope of bond taxation is too wide to cover in its entirety, we are going to focus on the more common tax implications.

When it comes to Treasuries, interest payments are taxed as ordinary income at the federal level, but are tax exempt at the state and local levels. This is an advantage over corporate bonds, which are taxed as ordinary income at all levels. We know that corporate bonds pay a default risk premium over Treasuries, but if you're holding the bonds in a fully taxable account, make sure the premium is big enough to compensate for the additional taxes. If it doesn't, then you're better of seeking the safety of Treasuries.

Municipal bonds are tax exempt at the federal level, and when issued by the state where you reside, are also tax exempt at the state and local levels. Finding a fund that specializes in muni bonds for the larger states, such as New York and California, isn't a challenge. These are readily available and the residents can earn a relatively safe yield without paying taxes. Vanguard also offers a selection of muni bond funds by state. If available for your state, these are a great way to avoid taxes when investing outside of a tax-deferred retirement account. But if you are investing in either a 401(k) or an IRA, there's no tax benefit to investing in municipal bonds, and Treasuries often pay higher interest.

Treasury Inflation Protected Securities, or TIPS, are the only bonds that truly offer protection against inflation, but they come with horrible tax consequences. The instrument pays a fixed rate of interest, yet the par value is indexed for inflation against the Consumer Price Index. If you're worried that your capital won't keep pace with inflation during the years when it matters the most, this is the security for you. TIPS are extremely popular amongst retirees. Here's how they work:

If we make a $500 investment with a fixed interest rate of 2%, and inflation over the first year is 3%, then the par value of your bond will be raised from $500 to $515. And the 2% interest yield is then applied against $515. If inflation keeps going up, so will the par value of the bond, and the fixed interest rate will continue to be applied against the higher value. But during periods of disinflation, the par value will be reduced. Let's say, for example, during the second year we experience disinflation of 2.5%, then the par value will be reduced from $515 to $502, and the 2% interest rate will now be applied to this amount.

It seems like a wonderful hedge against inflation. And on top of this, TIPS exhibit weak correlation with other asset classes. But the tax implications leave a lot to be desired. With most other bonds, the investor only pays capital gains tax if the bond is sold before maturity. With TIPS, capital gains tax is paid as the par value increases. For this reason, it's recommended that TIPS only be held inside a tax-deferred retirement account.

Given that our goal is to only invest in asset classes that have a history of beating inflation over the long-haul, there are some bond issues that should only be held in a retirement account. TIPS are a great example. But the same applies to T-bills. These are the lowest paying Treasuries because their duration is less than one year. They're priced to keep pace with inflation. But if held in a taxable account, the after-tax return is guaranteed to lag inflation. We know that bondholders demand a premium for any risk assumed beyond that of a T-bill. The longer the duration, the higher the premium. The same applies with default risk and exchange rate risk. But if you're going to pay a tax on the interest, then you also require a premium that allows the bond fund to beat inflation after taxes are paid. Some funds offer a high enough premium to accomplish this, while others do not.

As a rule of thumb, before investing in a bond fund take the current yield and multiply it by one minus your tax rate. Then compare it to the yield on a T-bill. If the fund yields 6% and you're in the 22% tax bracket, the calculation is as follows:

$$0.06 \times (1 - 0.22) = 0.0468$$

So if T-bills are yielding less than 4.68%, you'll still beat inflation after taxes are paid. But remember, 22% is your federal income tax rate. Depending on the bond and your location, state and local tax implications will differ. This is why tax planning for bonds is complicated. The investor who holds them in a retirement account, of course, does not need to develop a tax strategy. When juggling multiple accounts, there's a tradeoff. If the bond interest is taxable, it will be taxed at a higher rate than your qualified stock dividends. At the same time, you expect larger capital gains from your stocks, and there will be tax implications as we rebalance.

As a general rule, if the bond is tax-free, hold it in your fully taxable account. If it's a TIP, hold it in your retirement account.

Real Estate

REITs are a good candidate to hold in a fully taxable account. It all comes down to the fact that we're allowed to depreciate the base for tax purposes. This might sound confusing, but after we walk through an example, I think your eyes will widen at the possibilities. Let's start by comparing the tax implications of purchasing a rental property to investing in an individual stock. And then we'll take a look at how this works with a REIT index rather than a single property.

With both stocks and real estate you're taxed on the capital gains. In fact, there aren't many investments where you won't be taxed on the capital gains. Computing the tax is relatively simple. You take the amount you sold the asset for over the price you paid for it (or the base), and then apply the applicable tax rate. The only difference is that when you purchase real estate as a rental property, you get to depreciate the building over 27.5 years as a business expense. When you purchase a stock, it's not a business expense, it's an investment, and there's no depreciation.

For example, if you purchase a rental property for $300,000, you can take a tax deduction of $10,909 each year for the next 27.5 years.

300,000 / 27.5 = 10,909

It's a nice deduction that you'll want to take advantage of, but it's important to understand that as you depreciate the asset, you also lower the base. After the first year your $300,000 investment now has a $289,091 base. So if you wait two years and then sell it for $310,000, you'll be taxed on the difference of $31,818.

Year 1 depreciation: $10,909

Year 2 depreciation: $10,909

Total depreciation: $21,818

Base: 300,000 – 21,818 = 278,182

Capital gain: 310,00 – 278,182 = 31,818

If you hold the property for longer than 27.5 years and then sell it for $400,000, the entire $400,000 will be subject to capital gains tax. That's because depreciation lowers the base of the property. And in this example the base was lowered all the way down to zero. So what you're really doing is taking a tax deduction today that will be paid back when you sell the property.

If we go back to *Chapter 2: Compound Interest*, we know how the time value of money works. Each deduction that we take for a period of 27.5 years represents free cash flow that we can invest in something else. When it comes time to pay taxes on the full $400,000 we should be in a pretty good position. Sure, taxes hurt, but we're better off taking the depreciation now and paying the capital gains tax later.

If instead of investing in the rental property we put the full $300,000 into Microsoft Corporation (MSFT), there's no depreciation involved. The base remains at $300,000, and if we sell it down the road for $400,000, then we're only taxed on the $100,000 gain. Yes, it's a smaller tax liability on the back end, but we miss out on the free cash flow to invest in other assets during the period that we hold the stock.

When it comes to REITs, the buying and selling occurs within the trust, and the tax consequences are then passed along to the shareholders. You might receive a dividend of $2.50, but $0.75 of this might be considered a return of capital due to depreciation. In other words, you're not taxed on your share of the depreciation, and by labeling it a return of capital, your basis in the REIT is reduced by $0.75. It works just like a holding in a rental property, except it's being passed down to you. That's one huge advantage of investing in REITs over stocks. Taxes aren't paid on the entire dividend.

Another advantage of REITs over stocks is that the dividends are not subject to double taxation. In fact, the REIT hardly pays any tax at all. REITs are legally required to distribute 90% of their income in the form of a dividend.

And the tax burden is passed along with it. The plus side is that this causes REITs to offer some incredibly strong dividends. The downside is that investors don't receive preferential tax treatment on their dividends. The portion of the dividend that is not a return of capital will be taxed as ordinary income. And just to make the tax on a REIT distribution a little more complex, part of the dividend might be a capital gain. REITs don't just depreciate their properties, they also sell them. If the REIT has a capital gain, it is passed along to you in the dividend. Here, the treatment is the same as a capital gain on a stock. If the property was held for greater than one year it receives preferential treatment and is generally taxed at 15%. If the property was held less than one year it's taxed as ordinary income.

So what we're really looking at is a single dividend that needs to be divided into three parts, and each of those parts has a different tax implication. The part that consists of rental payments is taxed as ordinary income. The part that consists of depreciation (or a return of capital) is tax free. And the part that consists of capital gains is taxed as either a short-term or long-term capital gain depending on how long the property was held inside the REIT.

As income generating investments, REITs are a wonderful addition to the portfolio. They provide strong dividend yields and are good for diversification. And though the taxes might be complicated, it can work in the investor's favor. We avoid the double taxation that accompanies a stock investment. The return of capital is tax free. And the capital gain is eligible for preferential treatment. The only downside is that the rental payments and short-term capital gains are taxed as ordinary income.

If you want a good investment and don't mind making your tax accountant work a little harder, a REIT index serves as a wonderful addition to the portfolio. If you really want to make your accountant earn his pay, go ahead and add a foreign REIT index to the portfolio. It will keep him busy for hours. But if you keep your foreign REIT holdings in a tax deferred account, you not only do your accountant a favor, you also do yourself a favor. Foreign REITs are extremely tax inefficient. Many of the tax benefits on a domestic REIT do not apply in foreign countries where the real estate market is still developing. It's strongly encouraged that this type of investment only be held in a tax-deferred retirement account.

Conclusion

Returning to the notion of only controlling the things that can be controlled, it should be noted that every investor has some degree of control over their dividend yield. Even as we focus on growth in the early years, we still want to incorporate markets that pay dividends, and though we can't control the average yield provided by these markets at any given point in time, we can control whether or not we incorporate at least some allocation to higher yielding markets, such as REITs and the Dividend Aristocrats, into the portfolio. And we can similarly control how much we contribute to dividend paying funds at each stage in the investment lifecycle.

From a dividend perspective, the least amount of control comes from bonds. This is primarily due to the fact that the Federal Reserve has authority to lower the targeted fed funds rate during recessions or periods of declining growth. During the financial crisis of 2007-2008 the fed funds rate was reduced from its recent high of 5.25% in August of 2007 all the way down to 0.25% in December of 2008. For retirees who may have allocated greater than 60% of their portfolio to bonds, this reduction was catastrophic to their annual income. Yes, the average rents distributed on REITs also declined, but not by anything close to 95%. While the financial crises did take a toll on the housing market, people still needed a place to live, a somewhat staggering percentage of businesses continued to inhabit brick and mortar outlets, and to varying extents, forms of rent continued to be paid. As far as REITs are concerned, the higher the yield was to begin with, the higher the cut on average. Some reduced their distributions by as much as 25%, others by a smaller 15%. While material, it's nothing compared to a 95% reduction in the fed funds rate. The fact that the crisis was predicated on real estate is also significant, as the performance of REITs could be entirely different during the next stock market crash. As far as stocks are concerned, companies who prided themselves as Dividend Aristocrats—*and had the wherewithal to pay*—continued to increase their payments during the financial crises, while some of the more battered companies, such as Ford Motor Company (F), were forced to place their dividend on temporary hiatus. A well diversified stock investor saw little change. Dividends distributed by the SPDR Dow Jones Industrial Average ETF (DIA) continued as normal, with payments gradually increasing over time. What changed drastically was the yield when measured in terms of the current stock price. With stocks cut in half by March of 2009, the yield doubled, and any new money thrown into this market was handsomely rewarded. Of course, it's not necessary to catch these trends at the very bottom. A rebalancing strategy that consisted of stocks, bonds, and real estate would have insured that some profits were taken from bonds to buy both stocks and real estate at discount prices. The true benefits of rebalance are then granted to the long-term investor who sees the crash all the way through.

Certainly, we can't control for these types of events. What we can control for is how we react to them. The bond investor can control how long they hold their bond funds as rates are slashed. And we've seen that this is where long-term bonds become particularly valuable during retirement. With the exception of atypical economic conditions that create an inverted yield curve, long-term bonds will pay higher yields than short-term bonds, and the retired investor should use this to his advantage in order to increase interest payments. Given that the price of a bond is inversely related to yield, a long-term bond fund holds the greatest chances of appreciating in value during a recession. This gives the bondholder an opportunity to reduce his holdings at a profit, and reallocate his funds to markets that will continue to make distributions throughout the downturn. In all likelihood, a significant reduction in the fed funds rate will coincide with a bear market for stocks, as it did during the great recession, and this will allow the investor to reallocate his portfolio while stocks are selling at a discount.

We are not attempting to time the market and predict the direction of stocks. Instead, we are responding to an event that has already occurred. When the fed funds rate is reduced drastically it provides the opportunity to sell our long-term bond holdings at a profit and reallocate to higher yielding markets before the effect significantly impacts our interest payments. Stocks may continue to decline after the reallocation. Or maybe we'll get lucky and catch them at their bottom. It's a crapshoot that is beyond our control and our strategy should not be based on trying to obtain such control. It's simply out of reach. So we instead strive to mitigate the impact of that which is beyond our control. We want to maintain our level of passive income knowing that stocks will increase in value over the long-run. It's also important to note that we're not sacrificing capital in order to increase yield. Through our rebalancing strategy we would sell a portion of the bond funds regardless. But when rates get down around zero, and existing bonds spike in value, it makes sense to sell more than we normally would. We can control for this, and it helps keep our dividend yield intact.

The easiest element of investing to control for is our monthly contribution. Without savings you have nothing to invest. It's that simple. And while some investors tend to contribute more when markets are doing well (that is, when stocks are expensive but confidence is high), others tend to contribute more after the market has made a notable correction or entered bear territory. And while the merits of dollar cost averaging are heavily stressed over attempts to time the market, there is a benefit to contributing more when markets are down. Stocks are simply cheaper, and if you can skimp a bit on your normal spending habits and throw a little extra money at the market, then you're going to experience extraordinary results on the way back up. I applaud any extra dedication that investors make when markets are performing poorly, so long as it's just that—*extra effort*. When implementing a strategy based on dollar cost averaging, one should stick to their plan and not skip making investments in hopes of finding a more advantageous entry point. Sure, there will be times when they get lucky and find the entry point that they're looking for. But over the course of one's investing years there will be far more instances where markets keep going higher and higher and that advantageous entry point keeps getting farther and farther out of sight. This unfortunate turn of events will leave the investor with two choices: they can either throw in the towel and buy in at a higher price than would have been achieved through dollar cost averaging, or they can continue to wait as the price keeps going higher and higher. The longer they wait the higher the market can go, and the greater the chance of it turning against them after they finally succeed to buying in at a higher price. This is why dollar cost averaging is recommended, as it removes all guess-work from the equation.

Barring any sudden and unexpected changes in employment, you know what your income is going to be, and the cost of your lifestyle is within your control (*or perhaps this control is shared with a significant other!*). If the contribution is set at $6,000 annually, then a minimum of $500 needs to be invested each month in order to meet your goal. It's okay to contribute more, but never contribute less.

If you invest $8,000 this year but only $4,000 next year, it's not necessarily as good as investing $6,000 each of the two years. Yes, the time value of money dictates that a dollar invested today is worth more than a dollar invested tomorrow, but this rule is based on averages. If the market goes down this year and then up next year, would you want it going down against a $6,000 investment or against an $8,000 investment? And when it goes back up next year wouldn't you better off having thrown a fresh $6,000 at the market instead of only $4,000? If you don't contain a consistent minimum investment while dollar cost averaging then you're betting on luck, which isn't much different than attempting to time the market. It's okay to contribute more today than you have to, especially if markets are down. But if you throw in more than $6,000 (or whatever your number is) this year, it doesn't mean you should throw in less the following year. Failing to meet your minimum contribution can deteriorate the benefits of dollar cost averaging when markets don't behave as desired. I'm not an advocate of market timing, and I honestly believe that it's never a bad time to contribute more than necessary to the portfolio. But there are indeed times when it is more advantageous to make an extra contribution. It's difficult to predict in advance, but when an advantageous time to up the contribution arrives it will be really easy to spot. If the market is down 20% to 30% from its top, and you have greater than a five year investment horizon ahead of you, then it's an opportune time to throw some extra money at the market. It really doesn't get any simpler than that.

In fact, when bear markets are encountered I recommend cutting back on living expenses in order to purchase as many additional securities as possible. Sacrificing a couple nights on the town this month (and maybe next month, or even the next eleven months) can have a profound impact on your portfolio, and it will benefit you for the rest of your life.

While we know that we're going to hit a few bear markets over our investing career, we can't control when a crash will occur. But what we can do is control for the markets that we're invested in, and we've selected those markets based not only on their long-run historical returns, but also on their levels of risk (and safety).

It's okay if, at times, returns are less than expected, so long as you continue to contribute new capital, reinvest your dividends, and rebalance. As markets move through their cycles, rewards will be brought to you. The end goal is to build a stream of passive dividend income that you can live off of for the rest of your life. It's an ambitious yet achievable goal. In the introduction I made it a point to set reasonable expectations. The earlier you start investing, the more achievable the goal will be. The later in life you wait, the greater the likelihood that you will need other forms of income, such as social security, a pension, or a reverse mortgage on your home. Dividend income isn't the only way to secure a comfortable retirement. Any combination of approaches can be applied. And where the investment horizon is too short for dividend payments to compound in size to something that is self-sustaining, then building a smaller stream of passive dividend income to compliment your other income sources will further improve your position.

I hope you've enjoyed *Dividend Investing* and I hope you've benefited from the material. In *Chapter 6: Attributes to Consider When Selecting Stocks*, I acknowledged that there are as many different approaches to picking stocks as there are investors who pick them. The same observation can be applied to portfolio construction. As investors, we all have different tolerances for risk and different preferences in asset classes and subclasses. The more experienced reader might have an approach that differs from the material contained within. And the new investor should continue to read books on investing to ensure they develop an approach that works for them. Either way, I hope you're excited about implementing a strategy that will help you build wealth in the years to come.

Best of luck with your investments!

A Final Note to the Reader

Still have questions? That's fine. Investing can pose challenges. There is no single book that will answer all of your questions. Like anything in life, success with your investments is a process of continual learning followed by proper implementation. Don't just read one book about investing. Do what I do and read as many of them as you can.

We have plenty of resources available at www.theselfmadeinvestor.com. We offer tools to help you benchmark and rebalance your portfolio. We publish book recommendations for further reading. The books we recommend are the same books that I've learned from myself, and we only review books that will provide value to our readers. The blog posts, of course, are free. So there's no reason why a fee-conscious index fund investor wouldn't want to pay us a visit.

And if you still have questions, please feel free to shoot me an email: theselfmadeinvestor@gmail.com

As a self-published author I rely on reviews to sell my work. If you feel that the material presented in *Dividend Investing* will provide value to other readers, please leave a review on Amazon. Your support is greatly appreciated!

Made in United States
North Haven, CT
04 November 2026

21772133R00136